The World of Shells

Also in this series
The World of Butterflies
The World of Moths
The World of Minerals

The World of
SHELLS

Text by
Robert Scase

Photographs by
Eric Storey

Larousse & Co., Inc.,
New York

First published in the United States by
Larousse & Co., Inc.
572 Fifth Avenue
New York, New York 10036
1975

© Copyright 1975
Robert P. Scase and Eric S. Storey

All rights reserved

ISBN 0-88332-074-6 (Hardback Edition)
ISBN 0-88332-073-8 (Paperback Edition)
Library of Congress Catalog Card Number 75-1762

Printed in Great Britain

Dedicated to the late Marjory Paterson,
of Launceston, Tasmania, and formerly of
King Island, who sent the author the
'green snails' from Manus Island, and
whose love of the 'world of shells', of
'all things bright and beautiful' and
of her fellow mortals triumphed over
the rapid onset of total blindness, to
make her life an inspiration to us all.

Contents

Introduction ix
Definition ix
History ix
Classification of Mollusca x
Regions of the World xii
Life-history of Molluscs xiii
Enemies xv
Self-protection xv

Structure of the Animal xvi
The Shell xvii
Forming a Collection xix
Cleaning Shells xx
Looking After the Collection xxi
Shell Clubs and Societies xxi
Notes on the Headings xxii
Acknowledgments xxii

CEPHALOPODA
1 *Spirula spirula*
2 *Nautilus pompilius*
3 *Argonauta nodosa*

GASTROPODA
  Prosobranchia
4 *Patella longicosta*
5 *Perotrochus hirasei*
6 *Haliotis iris*
7 *Haliotis assimilis*
8 *Maurea cunninghami*
9 *Turbo chrysostomus*
10 *Turbo petholatus*
11 *Guilfordia yoka*
12 *Phasianella australis*
13 *Angaria delphinus*
14 *Epitonium scalare*
15 *Janthina prolongata*
16 *Carinaria lamarcki*
17 *Xenophora pallidula*
18 *Stellaria solaris*
19 *Architectonica trochlearis*
20 *Strombus aratrum*
21 *Strombus gallus*
22 *Strombus sinuatus*
23 *Strombus listeri*
24 *Strombus gigas*
25 *Lambis digitata*
26 *Lambis violacea*
27 *Tibia fusus*
28 *Terebellum terebellum*
29 *Ovulum ovum*
30 *Volva volva*
31 *Cypraea ocellata*
32 *Cypraea tessellata*
33 *Cypraea granulata*

34	Cypraea fultoni	74	Vexillum sanguisugum
35	Cypraea friendii	75	Afrivoluta pringlei
36	Cypraea aurantium	76	Oliva porphyria
37	Cypraea argus	77	Oliva reticulata
38	Cypraea mappa	78	Harpa major
39	Cypraea reevei	79	Harpa costata
40	Tonna perdix	80	Terebra subulata
41	Cypraecassis rufa	81	Conus marmoreus
42	Charonia tritonis	82	Conus imperialis
43	Biplex perca	83	Conus regius
44	Bursa candisata	84	Conus ammiralis
45	Murex tribulus	85	Conus generalis
46	Murex cornutus	86	Conus geographus
47	Murex alatus	87	Conus aulicus
48	Murex palmarosae	88	Conus bengalensis
49	Murex cervicornis	89	Conus textile
50	Murex burnetti	90	Conus adamsonii
51	Murex cichoreus	91	Conus nussatella
52	Murex scorpio	92	Conus granulatus
53	Trophon catalinensis	93	Columbarium pagoda
54	Trophon geversianum	94	Thatcheria mirabilis
55	Latiaxis mawae		Opisthobranchia
56	Latiaxis tosanus	95	Aplustrum amplustre
57	Latiaxis lischkeana		Pulmonata
58	Busycon contrarium	96	Papustyla pulcherrima
59	Melongena corona	97	Polymita picta
60	Voluta ebraea	98	Liguus fasciatus
61	Lyria kurodai		
62	Lyria lyraeformis		
63	Cymbiola cymbiola		
64	Cymbiola imperialis		
65	Cymbiola nivosa		BIVALVIA (or PELECYPODA)
66	Harpulina arausiaca	99	Neotrigonia margaritacea
67	Volutoconus bednalli	100	Spondylus americanus
68	Volutoconus grossi	101	Gloripallium pallium
69	Scaphella junonia	102	Brechites pulcher
70	Scaphella dubia	103	Chama lazarus
71	Amoria undulata	104	Corculum cardissa
72	Mitra papalis	105	Amiantis erycina
73	Vexillum regina	106	Tellina radiata

Introduction

Definition

What is a shell? In the present book the term is used for the hard, rigid structure enclosing the whole body, or occasionally just some part of the body, of a soft-bodied creature known as a mollusc. During its lifetime the shell protects the animal and supports it, just as our skeletons support our own bodies, and it too is left behind when the animal dies. The skeletons of mammals are functional, but could hardly be called beautiful, whereas the shells of many molluscs are among the most beautiful of Nature's creations.

History

From fossil evidence, shells are thought to have been present on this planet for at least 400 million years – a much longer period than man himself – and some of the present-day shells bear a striking resemblance to their primitive ancestors, so much so that the term 'living fossils' could well be applied to them. In most fossils no trace of the original colour is present, but it seems probable that they were just as colourful as those which survive and give us so much pleasure today.

Shells are some of the earliest natural objects known to have been collected by man, and it has been surmised that the cowry shell in particular had a certain sexual symbolism for our prehistoric ancestors. The shell cult was very widespread, being known from places as far apart as the Mediterranean and parts of Central and South America. Because of their beauty, shells were sometimes used (and still are at the present day) for personal adornment, and because of their convenient size, either in their natural form or when fashioned into artefacts, some were also widely used as currency in many parts of the world, notably in Africa, in North America and in some Pacific islands.

Artists found inspiration in their forms and colours as early as the fourteenth century, but the first great work devoted entirely to illustrations of shells was the *Historia Conchyliorum* by Martin Lister (published 1685–92). This gave a great impetus to the hobby of shell-collecting, or conchology[1], as it came to be known, a hobby the pursuit of which was a direct result of the great voyages of discovery to such places as the New World and the East Indies. Cabinets of 'Natural Curiosities' were fashionable throughout Europe during the Renaissance, and contained many shells. With the arrival of good books on them, interest was stimulated still further, and the first work with coloured plates appeared in 1755. The publication of the *Systema Naturae* by Linnaeus in 1735 had already given the collector a simple method of labelling specimens, two Latin names being sufficient to identify any particular shell and distinguish it from nearly-related species.

During the nineteenth century many famous shell collections came into being, and the libraries of collectors were enriched with some excellent, beautifully illustrated but expensive books. From time to time auctions of shells were held, and high prices were sometimes paid for rare specimens. Nevertheless, by the close of the century the hobby was already declining in popularity, possibly because many collectors had turned to philately and were finding that stamp albums took up less room than shell cabinets. Since the Second World War, however, perhaps because of the increasing use of the aqualung and skin-diving techniques, there has been a world-wide revival of interest, both in shells and in the living molluscs which create them, and universal recognition that we should make every effort to safeguard and conserve this rich heritage for future generations.

Classification of Mollusca

The molluscs form one of the major groups, or *phyla*, which make up the animal kingdom, and possibly total something like 90,000 species. The phylum Mollusca is subdivided into seven *classes*, only three of which are represented in this volume. These are the *Cephalopoda* (including active animals, such as the nautilus, the octopus and the squid), the *Bivalvia* or *Pelecypoda* (bivalves, such as the oyster and scallop) and the *Gastropoda* (snail-like creatures which crawl along on a foot). The remaining classes of the Mollusca are the *Aplacophora* (solenogasters, worm-like, lacking a shell), the *Monoplacophora* (gastroverms, very

[1] Pronounced 'konkology'.

primitive, limpet-like and only recently discovered), the *Amphineura* (chitons or coat-of-mail shells) and the *Scaphopoda* (tusk shells) — all comparatively small groups, highly specialized and of limited appeal to the average collector.

Within the larger *classes* there are numerous *families*, and the families represented in this book are listed here. They contain most of the shells which are renowned for their beauty:

CLASS CEPHALOPODA
- *Spirulidae* (ram's-horn shell)
- *Argonautidae* (argonauts or paper nautilus)
- *Nautilidae* (nautilus shells)

CLASS GASTROPODA
Sub-class 1. Prosobranchia
- *Patellidae* (limpets)
- *Pleurotomariidae* (slit shells)
- *Haliotidae* (abalones or ormers)
- *Trochidae* (top shells)
- *Turbinidae* (turban shells)
- *Phasianellidae* (pheasant shells)
- *Angariidae* (dolphin shells)
- *Epitoniidae* (wentle traps)
- *Janthinidae* (violet sea-snails)
- *Carinariidae* (carinarias)
- *Xenophoridae* (carrier shells)
- *Architectonicidae* (sundial shells)
- *Strombidae* (conchs or strombs)
- *Ovulidae* (egg cowries)
- *Cypraeidae* (cowries)
- *Tonnidae* (tun shells)
- *Cassidae* (helmet shells)
- *Cymatiidae* (tritons)
- *Bursiidae* (frog shells)
- *Muricidae* (rock shells)
- *Magilidae* (coral shells)
- *Buccinidae* (whelks and crown conchs)
- *Volutidae* (volutes)
- *Mitridae* (mitre shells)
- *Marginellidae* (margin shells)

Olividae	(olive shells)
Harpidae	(harp shells)
Terebridae	(auger shells)
Conidae	(cone shells)
Columbariidae	(pagoda shells)
Turridae	(turrid shells)

Sub-class 2. Opisthobranchia
    Hydatinidae   (bubble shells)

Sub-class 3. Pulmonata
    Helicidae
    Orthalicidae

CLASS BIVALVIA (PELECYPODA)

Trigoniidae	(brooch shells)
Spondylidae	(thorny oysters)
Pectinidae	(scallops)
Clavagellidae	(watering-pot shells)
Chamidae	(jewel boxes)
Cardiidae	(cockles)
Veneridae	(venus clams)
Tellinidae	(wedge shells)

Other large families, which are *not* represented in the following pages, include the *Fissurellidae* (keyhole limpets), *Neritidae* (nerites), *Naticidae* (moon shells), *Littorinidae* (periwinkles), *Turritellidae* (screw shells), *Cerithiidae* (ceriths), *Fasciolariidae* (tulip shells), *Fusinidae* (spindle shells), *Cancellariidae* (nutmeg shells) and many bivalve families.

The families are further divided into *genera*, and the genera into *species*. The two Latin names which identify a shell consist of the *generic name* followed by the *specific name*. To make it complete, the name (often abbreviated) of the author (the person who first described the shell) should be added after the specific name used by that author.

Regions of the World

For the purpose of mapping the distribution of both sea shells and land shells, it is convenient to divide the earth's surface into definite geographical regions, where the composition of the molluscan fauna is characteristic of those particular areas. These are known as *provinces*, and the names of a great number of these are self-explanatory (e.g. in the marine provinces such names as Californian, Peruvian, West African,

Arctic and Mediterranean). Other names need some explanation, and the following notes should help:

The *Indo-Pacific Province* is a vast region embracing the whole of the Indian Ocean, the East Indies and Philippines, and most of the Pacific Ocean between 30°N. and 30°S., including Hawaii and Easter Island, but not reaching the American coastline. It includes all the northern half of Australia.

The *Mediterranean* (or *Lusitanian*) *Province* not only covers the Mediterranean, but also that part of the Atlantic Ocean from the Bay of Biscay to north-west Africa.

The *Carolinian* (or *Transatlantic*) *Province* extends down the Atlantic coast of America from Cape Cod to northern Florida.

The *Caribbean Province* continues from southern Florida south as far as Rio de Janeiro in Brazil.

The *Panamic Province* stretches from California to Ecuador.

The *Australian Province* consists of the southern half of Australia, with Tasmania, and the whole of New Zealand.

The *Japonic Province* covers central Japan and the east coast of Korea.

Life History of Molluscs

The Molluscan Egg All molluscs start life as an egg. Within this egg a tiny shell develops even before hatching takes place, though it may bear little resemblance to the adult shell. The eggs may be laid singly or in clusters, or in the case of many marine gastropods in capsules, which may be hard or soft and may take various forms, each capsule containing a quantity of eggs. In certain marine molluscs the egg masses may take the form of twisted ribbons wound in a spiral, or of overlapping plates. They are normally laid in shallow water, and some molluscs, such as the cowries, will sit on the eggs for several days. The number of eggs laid by a marine mollusc during a single spawning may exceed a million, to compensate for a very high mortality rate after hatching, or may be as low as several hundred. Land and fresh-water mollusca deposit far fewer eggs, usually near the surface of the soil or on leaves, and development reaches a more advanced stage before hatching takes place, a few species being viviparous. One land snail from South America lays eggs as large as a pigeon's egg, with a hard shell.

Trochophore (or Trochosphere) The first free-swimming larval stage of the marine molluscs is known as the trochophore. Like the next stage it is planktonic, drifting freely with ocean currents, and is characterized by a ring of fine 'hairs' or cilia encircling the body just in front of the mouth.

Veliger Within a short space of time the trochophore is transformed into the veliger larva, in which the ciliated bands have increased in size and complexity, forming a fringe on the edges of a circular or lobed organ termed the 'velum', to assist in collecting food and in swimming. Certain organs which characterize the adult stage, such as the mantle, the foot and the shell, are now recognizable.

Only a tiny fraction of the vast numbers of veligers in the ocean ever reaches maturity. The veliger stage may last for a very short period – a matter of hours – or for several months, and it is during this time that it may be carried considerable distances by ocean currents, thus helping the dispersal of the species. As the shell of the veliger continues to grow, the term 'veliconcha' is sometimes used to describe the stage reached, and the shell is now termed a 'protoconch'.

The Juvenile Stage The mollusc is now no longer free-swimming, and it develops the habits of the adult form, crawling if it is a gastropod, or settling down in one spot or burrowing in the case of most bivalves. The shell, however, is frequently very different from the adult shell, both in colour and in form. A collection of a series of growth stages of any shell is most valuable and instructive.

The Adult Some molluscs reach maturity in one year and then die; many, however, live much longer. A normal figure for many marine gastropods would be about five years, and such shells as the giant clams, which occur on the Great Barrier Reef and in other parts of the Pacific, may attain a considerable age. It has even been suggested that, given favourable conditions, they may live for the best part of a century. The mature shell may be just a larger version of the juvenile stage, but in many gastropods there may be a thickening of the lip of the shell (as in the strombs), and in the case of the cowries there is a complete change of shape, accompanied by a different colour pattern.

Molluscs may be hermaphrodite (i.e. both sexes may be present in the same individual) as in the land snails, or in some cases there may be a change of sex from male to female during the animal's lifetime, but in most marine molluscs the sexes are separate and remain so throughout life, and some exhibit sexual dimorphism, the shell of the female often being larger than that of the male. Aside from any sexual differences, in some molluscs the adult shell may vary considerably in size, even in a single species, depending to some extent on the environment. Whatever the size, however, the onset of maturity results in spawning, which may happen only once a year or with some species over a long period of time. It is frequently a communal affair, large numbers of the same type of shell congregating at one spot. With the hatching of the eggs the whole cycle starts over again.

Enemies

The enemies of the soft-bodied molluscs surround them on every side. In the young stages of the marine species the veligers swarm in shallow water on sunny days and provide food for many of the animals which feed on such drifting plankton. In the adult state many molluscs are carnivorous, and prey upon each other. Such fish as the cod and the mussel-cracker take their toll, as do the sea-birds, and on land also many snails are eaten by birds, such as the thrush.

As in other fields, however, it is man himself who now poses one of the worst threats to the survival of the shell population, whether it be by polluting the environment with chemicals, by destruction of coral reefs to build airfields or hotels, by drainage of marshy ground, by commercial exploitation of rare species, involving large-scale dredging and subsequent selling of the shells for profit, or by the thoughtless actions of many private collectors who destroy shell habitats and over-collect in their efforts to improve their own collections.

Self-protection

Various devices are adopted by molluscs to enable them to survive. One such device is camouflage of the shell, and this can be very effective. Some shells are disguised by a thick, chalky deposit which renders them almost invisible when viewed from above. Many brightly coloured shells, such as cone-shells and conchs, have a tough fibrous or horny coating, known as the *periostracum*, which completely hides the colours beneath, though this may be incidental. In the cowries part of the body of the animal can be extended to cover the shell when the animal is in motion. The carrier shells cement small stones or pieces of coral or other shells to their upper surface, until they are no longer recognizable as shells. The violet sea snails, which drift on the surface of the ocean, have their own colour scheme to render them inconspicuous, both from above and below.

Some molluscs when in danger will amputate a portion of their foot, which serves to distract the would-be predator while the inhabitant of the shell makes its escape. Some of the cephalopods emit an inky fluid, which acts as a 'smoke screen'.

Many of the land snails and marine shells close the aperture of the shell with a 'trap-door', or *operculum*, after retreating inside it, or the mouth of the shell may be permanently constricted by the formation of 'teeth' or projections, leaving just room for their own bodies to emerge, but serving as an effective barrier against would-be attackers. The spiny projections which are such a conspicuous feature on the outside of certain shells would be an effective deterrent in the event of any predator attempting to make a meal of them.

Structure of the Animal

Gastropods Generally speaking, the animals of most of the gastropods resemble the snail which is so familiar in our gardens. They crawl along by a 'rippling' motion of the underside of the foot. On the head are tentacles, two pairs being usual, which serve as organs of touch. The eyes may be situated at the tip of the tentacles or on the head near the base of the tentacles. The organ which is most characteristic of the gastropods, however, is the structure known as the *radula*, which is used in feeding. It is ribbon-like and bears many teeth in parallel rows, with which it rasps away the outer layers of its food, be it animal or vegetable. The shape of the teeth and their arrangement on the radula are very important in classification. The tube-like organ which bears the radula in some molluscs is termed the *proboscis*, or snout: it can be very elastic, and in the case of some of the carnivorous species it may be used to inject a poison into the victim. Another tube-like structure in the marine gastropods is the *siphon*, through which fresh water for breathing is drawn into the body. Respiration may be by means of gills in the aquatic species, or by a simple type of lung in the land snails. There is a typical blood system in molluscs, with a heart, arteries and veins, the blood being colourless or very pale blue in colour.

The soft fleshy or membraneous layer of the animal which lines the shell in molluscs is termed the *mantle*. It is attached to the body near the apex of the shell, but inside the larger portion of the shell it is separated from the body by the *mantle cavity*, and becomes thickened into a sort of collar at the aperture. One of the chief functions of this part of the mantle is to create the shell itself, its cells extracting chemicals from the environment for this purpose. The cells of the edge of the mantle secrete pigments and lay down the colour pattern. In cowries the mantle can emerge from the shell as two 'flaps', which may completely cover the shell as the animal crawls along, and can be partially or wholly retracted by the animal. A powerful muscle enables most gastropods to retreat within their shells at will, or in such shells as the limpet to cling tightly to the rocks when disturbed.

Bivalvia Bivalves occur in the sea and in fresh water, but have not colonized the land. Most of them are sedentary in their habits, and as their movements are restricted there is no need for a head with eyes, tentacles and a radula. There are *two* siphons, and feeding is accomplished by the animal taking in water through one siphon, straining minute food particles from the water by means of the gills and expelling the water through the other siphon. There is a mouth to which the food particles are then swept along by the movement of tiny 'hairs', or *cilia*. A few bivalves, such as scallops and giant clams, have numerous eyes set into the edge of the mantle.

There is a well-developed foot which is *not* used for crawling but is modified for burrowing in mud or sand, and in some species enables the animal to bore into wood or even rocks. Scallops can swim actively for short periods by opening the valves of the shell and suddenly closing them, this action helping them to escape from such enemies as starfish by 'jet propulsion'. The mantle in bivalves consists of two equal halves, each of which forms one valve of the shell.

Cephalopoda These are wholly marine, and are the most highly developed of the mollusca. They have a well-developed head surrounded by a ring of prehensile tentacles, and can swim actively by expelling water from the mantle cavity through a funnel or siphon. The mouth is furnished with a horny beak as well as a radula. The eyes are large and often very complex. The shell may be external, but is often internal or more frequently entirely absent.

The Shell

The pages which follow this Introduction reveal a little of the beauty of individual shells. They also give some idea of the amazing assortment of different shapes, colour patterns and types of sculpture which combine to make molluscan shells so attractive to the collector. Quite apart from these individual differences, however, there are some general aspects of shells which need to be understood to appreciate them fully.

The shell in a few cephalopods and many gastropods is basically a *tube*, which lengthens and increases in diameter as the animal grows, and simultaneously often assumes a spiral form. This coiling takes place in a *clockwise* direction in the majority of gastropods, and such shells are said to be *dextral*. If held in the hand with the *apex*, or point from which growth starts, uppermost and the aperture towards one, then the aperture will be on the right-hand side. *Sinistral* shells coil in an *anticlockwise* direction, and if held in the same manner the aperture is on the left. A few marine shells and many land snails are *normally* sinistral, and in some of the land snails about half the individuals of a single species may coil one way and half the other. Where a species is normally dextral, sinistral forms are often highly prized.

The individual turns of these coiled shells are known as *whorls*, and they frequently overlap each other to form a conical *spire*, the last whorl, which is often much bigger than the preceding ones, being known as the *body whorl*. The coiling often results in a central pillar, known as the *columella*, which is only partially visible where it forms one side of the aperture. This portion of the shell can be prolonged into a hollow 'spike', sometimes referred to as the *siphonal canal*, as it surrounds the siphon and protects it. The columella may be hollowed out at its base, forming an *umbilicus*.

In some gastropods growth of the shell is not continuous, there being periodic resting stages during which no lengthening of the 'tube' takes place, but a thickening of the *lip* or edge of the aperture occurs, sometimes taking the form of a 'frill' or a row of spines. Growth is then resumed, so that a *rib* is left around the whorl: these ribs or frilly projections marking the position of former apertures are known as *varices*. In some instances the shape of the shell changes completely when it becomes fully adult, usually because of some modification to the lip of the shell, which may develop claw-like processes or a flaring outline, or strong tooth-like projections within the aperture. In the adult cowries the body whorl is all that is visible, the spire of the juvenile shell being 'absorbed' within it and the 'teeth' bordering the slit-like aperture becoming very prominent: they are an important feature in classification.

In *bivalves* the two halves of the shell are joined by a *ligament*, which tends to force the valves apart, and a *hinge*, the shape of the hinge in these shells being one of the principal characters used to establish their identity. Each valve grows outwards from a portion near the hinge which is known as the *umbo*, the extreme tip of which is referred to as the *beak*. When the animal is removed, the inside of each valve is seen to bear either one or two scars, where the muscles which close the shell are attached.

The majority of shells consist largely of carbonate of lime, in the form of calcite or arragonite. This is deposited by the cells of the mantle in three distinct layers, a fact which makes it possible to carve cameos from certain shells. The nacreous, iridescent inner layer is often called 'mother-of-pearl'. The periostracum, a horny protective layer on the outside which has already been mentioned, frequently constitutes a fourth layer. The colour pattern of the mature shell, which is incorporated in the outermost of the three layers, is quite different from that of the immature shell, which can lead to some confusion unless one studies a growth series.

The *operculum* in gastropods, already mentioned under 'Self-protection', is not strictly part of the shell: it is a horny or calcareous plate attached to the foot and is roughly the same shape as the aperture. Where present, however, it should always be preserved by gumming it to some cotton-wool, which is then pushed into the aperture until as little of the cotton-wool as possible can be seen behind the operculum. The shell *with* the operculum is regarded by collectors as more complete, and therefore more valuable.

Forming a Collection

Sea shells may be collected in several ways:

(a) *By searching for them* on beaches and on coral reefs, by skin-diving or using an aqualung, or by dredging from a boat. All these methods probably give the maximum enjoyment to most collectors, because there is always a feeling of expectancy and the hope of finding something new. *It cannot be stressed too much* that all stones, coral boulders, etc., which are turned over should be returned to their former positions during the search. No imperfect live shells should be collected – the molluscs should be left to breed – and one should always remember the serious consequences of over-collecting in one area. Notes on the living animals and photographs of them are always of great value, as so little is known about many of them.

(b) *By buying shells* from dealers or at auctions. This can be expensive, but is often the only way of obtaining some rare shells, and one can build up a fine collection by such means if one can afford it. Excellent lists are obtainable from most dealers, and auction catalogues can usually be obtained in advance. It pays to keep in touch with the local museums: sometimes collections are offered to them which they do not want.

(c) *By exchange* with other collectors. One must first have shells to exchange, obtained by methods (a) or (b). It entails much time-consuming correspondence, but this in itself can be both enjoyable and helpful. One should never send poor material in exchanges, and always be prepared to return shells or give more in exchange for them, to ensure that *both* parties are satisfied with the deal.

(d) By *asking friends* travelling abroad to send back parcels of shells, with full details of where they were collected.

(e) By *obtaining shells from fishermen* in port. Many rare deep-water shells have been recovered from the stomachs of fish.

The technique of collecting *land* shells and *fresh-water* shells is different, but paragraphs (b), (c) and (d) are still applicable.

Cleaning Shells

Freezing and boiling are two methods frequently used for killing living molluscs. In the former case they should be thawed out *gradually* after freezing for several days, and if the second method is used then the water should *slowly* be brought to the boil and afterwards be allowed to cool gradually. Sudden temperature changes can cause cracks in the surface of shells with a high polish. A method which is preferable to either of the above with marine species, if it is desired to minimize any risk of damage to the shell, is to leave them in a closed vessel containing sea-water until the water becomes stale and death ensues, but if an aquarium is available the opportunity should always be taken to observe the living animal and make notes of its appearance and habits.

Once the animal is dead the soft parts are hooked out carefully, or flushed out with a strong jet of water. This is much easier if the shells have been placed, aperture uppermost, somewhere where they can be left for a week or two until the flesh starts to decay. To deodorize shells where repeated syringings have failed to remove the last traces of the animal, a few drops of formaldehyde may be inserted into the shell, held apex downwards, and the aperture is then plugged with cotton-wool. Bivalve shells will gape after death, and a knife may be used to remove the animal.

If it is desired to remove the periostracum, the shell may be immersed in a 10% solution of caustic potash, taking out the shell with tongs (*not* with the fingers) after a few minutes and holding it under a tap, then scrubbing it to see if the periostracum has softened sufficiently to come away easily, and repeating the process until it does so. Where marine growths render a specimen unsightly, they may be removed with a scrubbing brush or carefully prised away with a sharp instrument, after first soaking the shell in a strong solution of household bleach for twenty-four hours and then giving the shell a thorough wash. The periostracum may also be removed by this method. Acid should *never* be used on shells, as it will damage the surface.

Looking After the Collection

One should always aim to improve the quality of the shells in one's collection, and never be satisfied with worn and bleached 'beach' shells when they can be replaced by better ones. Live-collected shells are best for quality, and in the case of some of the cowries even these will begin to fade in a matter of weeks. The colours of all shells will fade if they are exposed to bright light: they are best kept in the dark.

As much collecting data as possible should accompany each shell, preferably written in Indian ink on a stout paper or card label. If this is placed *with the shell* in a glass-topped or plastic box or similar receptacle the chance of them becoming separated will be lessened. This is important if the collection is to have any scientific value. When exchanging shells, all such details should also be sent, if known. Many collections are housed in wooden or metal cabinets with shallow drawers of varying depths, and with the shells resting on blue or black cotton-wool or coloured foam-rubber within the boxes. Very small shells are best kept in glass tubes plugged with cotton-wool (*not* corked).

Certain shells lose much of their beauty when they are dry. Some collectors treat these, and also beach shells, with a *very thin* layer of vaseline or a mixture of one part of mineral oil and five parts of naphtha or lighter fuel, to restore their lustre. Varnish should *never* be used, however, and most forms of 'beauty treatment' for shells should be kept to a minimum. The above treatments should not be used in tropical climates, as they will encourage the growth of fungi, which can cause permanent damage to the shells.

Shells Clubs and Societies

All collectors are strongly advised to join a shell club or society if they wish to get the maximum benefit from their hobby. Such organizations are to be found in many parts of the world, and their number is growing as the hobby becomes ever more popular. Quite a number issue publications, some being well illustrated. One of their most useful functions is to keep one in touch with other collectors and with events in the shell world, such as the discovery of new species or the issue of new books. Some societies organize shell auctions, and regular meetings are held at which one can meet others with similar interests. A useful list of 'Shell

Clubs Around the World' has been compiled by the American Malacological Union.

Notes on the Headings

Scientific name Where a name is included in brackets between the generic and specific names, this is the subgeneric name. It is frequently used *in place of* the generic name in literature, and in such large genera as Murex and Conus it is sometimes accorded generic status.

Size Where two figures are given, it must not be assumed that these are maximum and minimum sizes for that particular species. However, it may be assumed that most adult specimens collected will fall somewhere between these two sizes. The size given is the measurement of the shell, including any spines, at its longest or widest point, *whichever is the greater*.

In the illustrations to this book a uniform scale has not been used, even for related species, so the reader should note the actual size.

Acknowledgments

The authors wish to express their gratitude to the following for providing specimens for illustration: Mr. H. C. Gay (one specimen of *Conus ammiralis*), Mr. W. Karo (*Charonia tritonis, Murex burnetti, Lyria kurodai* and *Spondylus americanus*), Mr. A. P. H. Oliver (*Murex tribulus*) and Mr. J. D. Orr (*Cypraea fultoni* and *Conus bengalensis*). All other specimens illustrated are from the collection of R. P. Scase.

The authors are also very grateful to the Trustees of the British Museum (Natural History) and to the Staff of the Mollusca Section there for providing facilities for studying their collections, and for access to literature.

CENTIMETRE SCALE

1 *Scientific name* Spirula spirula

Family Spirulidae

Common name Ram's-horn Shell

Size 2·0–2·5 cm.

Range World-wide in warm seas.

The animal which creates these delicate shells is a common cephalopod, allied to the cuttle-fish, and lives at depths between 600 and 3,000 feet. It normally floats or swims with its eight short arms and two longer tentacles hanging downwards, and the shell is totally enclosed within the upper one-third of its body. The shell is divided into two or three dozen chambers by a series of partitions, and this, together with a special laminated type of shell structure employed by the mollusc, results in a shell which, despite its delicate appearance, can withstand enormous changes of pressure as the animal ascends and descends in the ocean.

On the uppermost portion of the animal's body is a special organ emitting a greenish phosphorescent light, which it can do almost continuously, and may help to keep a shoal of these creatures together.

2 *Scientific name* Nautilus pompilius

Family Nautilidae

Common name Pearly Nautilus

Size 10–15 cm., but can exceed 20 cm.

Range South-west Pacific only

Nautiluses, of which there are six species today, are the only survivors of a group which was abundant in the oceans millions of years ago. Like the *Spirula*, the shell is chambered, but here it is an *external* shell, the cephalopod building a series of partitions behind its body as it grows and living inside the final or largest chamber, with its numerous short arms protruding from the aperture. The whole shell is shown on the left above, and a section of the shell in the centre.

As in *Spirula*, the chambers of the shell are connected by a small hole in each partition or *septum*, shown on the right, where most of the last chamber has been cut away. Through the holes passes a tubular extension of the body known as the *siphuncle*. It is thought that this may be used to adjust the pressure of gases within the shell to equal the pressure outside. Food, in the shape of crabs, shrimps, etc., is sought on the sea-bed, and the nautilus, which is a nocturnal animal, can crawl around and can also swim by a gentle form of 'jet propulsion', expelling water by contractions of its 'funnel'. It can close the entrance to its shell with a leather-like 'hood'.

3 *Scientific name* Argonauta nodosa
Family Argonautidae
Common name Paper Nautilus
Size 10–20 cm.
Range World-wide in warm seas

This fragile creation, though found in many shell collections, is not a true shell, but a protective 'cradle' for the eggs, formed by the female cephalopod and clasped to her body by two membraneous discs which have secreted the calcium carbonate of which it is formed, and which are actually modified arms. Her body is inside the 'shell' but there is no other attachment to it, and if removed from it she will not form another shell, but will die. The double row of brown knobs on the 'keel' of the shell are formed by the suckers of the arms. The male has no shell, and is only about 2 cm. long.

Another species – *Argonauta argo* – is perhaps even more common in warm seas, including the Mediterranean. Here the 'lumps' which are so conspicuous on the above shell are absent, and the parallel ridges are therefore more conspicuous.

4 *Scientific name* *Patella longicosta*
Family Patellidae
Common name Long-ribbed or Spiked Limpet
Size 5–7 cm.
Range South Africa

This is one of the most attractive of the limpets, with its deeply corrugated upper surface, each of the ribs projecting from the edge of the shell like the rays of a star. The beautifully enamelled under-surface, wherein lies the chief attraction of this group of shells, exhibits the usual scar in the centre, where a powerful muscle is attached, which enables the animal to cling tightly to the rocks. Many limpets browse on the algae which grow on the rocks around them, but return to the same spot at every low tide. Although limpet shells are conical and not coiled, the animals are typical gastropods, with a head bearing tentacles. They are abundant where they occur, and many of the finest species come from South Africa.

Key-hole limpets (Fissurellidae) are an allied family, distinguished by having a small hole at the apex of the shell.

5 *Scientific name* Perotrochus hirasei
Family Pleurotomariidae
Common name Emperor's Slit-shell
Size 8–12 cm.
Range Deep water off Japan

Before 1856 the slit shells were known only as fossils, having been abundant some 500 million years ago. Since then about sixteen living species have been discovered – all from deep water and all rare, though this one less so than the others. The slit, which in other species may be much longer than the one illustrated, enables the animal to get rid of its waste products without them passing over the gills. As the edge of the aperture, where the slit commences, grows onwards, so the other end of the slit is continually being filled with the same material as the rest of the shell, leaving a characteristic band around each whorl.

Any specimens found were once presented to the Emperor of Japan – hence the popular name.

6 *Scientific name*   *Haliotis iris*

Family   Haliotidae

Common name   Paua, or Rainbow Shell

Size   Up to 15 cm., occasionally more

Range   New Zealand and Chatham Is.

The members of this family are known variously as sea-ears, abalones or ormers in different parts of the world. The spiral shell is much flattened, a shape which enables the animal to cling tightly, like a limpet, to the underside of rocky ledges and boulders, at or below low-tide mark, where it feeds on the plant life. The row of holes serves the same purpose as the slit in the slit-shells (see previous page), water being expelled through them after passing over the gills, and as further holes are formed with the growth of the shell so the earlier holes are filled in, leaving from four to six holes open all the time.

In this species the predominant colours of the pearly interior are blues and greens, and the shells of the paua and its relatives in other lands are frequently used in the manufacture of costume jewellery. The outside of the shell is often thickly encrusted with marine growths.

7 *Scientific name*   *Haliotis assimilis*
Family   Haliotidae
Common name   Threaded Abalone
Size   10–13 cm.
Range   California

This species of abalone exhibits a large number of colour forms, of which the centre one depicted above is rare and most unusual. Here the 'cords' or 'threads' on the outside of the shell, from which it gets its name, are picked out in red and white. Other colour forms may have broad alternate bands of orange and white, or blue and reddish-brown crossing the cords at right angles. The colours are said to be partly the result of what type of food is available at any time, but in this species it is likely that heredity also plays a part.

    Abalones, or ormers, have for centuries been valued as an article of food, especially by the Chinese, and soups and chowders made from them are popular in California.

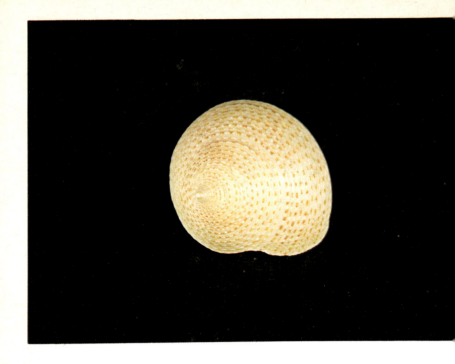

8 *Scientific name*   *Maurea cunninghami*

Family   Trochidae

Common name   Cunningham's Top Shell

Size   4–6 cm.

Range   New Zealand, more frequent in the south

Top shells, of which there are over a thousand species from both tropical and temperate seas, are very variable, but are characterized by this conical shape and by the presence of a circular horny operculum. The group of top shells known as Calliostomas, to which this shell is closely related, are mostly from colder seas, where some are found among beds of seaweed in fairly deep water. This particular species is often found on sandy ocean beaches, where its delicate colouring, with the fine beading on the ribs, harmonizes beautifully with its surroundings.

Scientific name   Turbo chrysostomus
Family   Turbinidae
Common name   Gold-mouthed Turban Shell
Size   5–7 cm.
Range   Indo-Pacific

Turban shells are similar to top shells in many respects, but instead of being thin and horny the operculum is thick, heavy and calcareous. These shells are frequent on coral reefs, the animals feeding on the plant life in shallow water. The interior of the shells is usually iridescent, being lined with nacre, or 'mother-of-pearl', and in this common species the nacre inside the aperture is of a wonderful golden hue, while in an allied species, the Silver-mouthed Turban, the silvery interior makes an interesting comparison.

10 *Scientific name* Turbo petholatus

Family Turbinidae

Common name Tapestry or Cat's-eye Turban Shell

Size 4–7 cm.

Range Indo-Pacific

The most popular of all the Turban Shells because of its high polish, its lovely and varied patterns and its beautiful colour schemes, which combine to make a series of these shells a revelation to all who see them. The solid operculum, about 2 cm. across, is the well-known 'cat's-eye', the glossy convex outer side deep blue-green, ringed with a paler band which is burnt orange on one side and white on the other, and is in great demand for costume jewellery. This species is found on the seaward side of coral reefs, where the water is shallow.

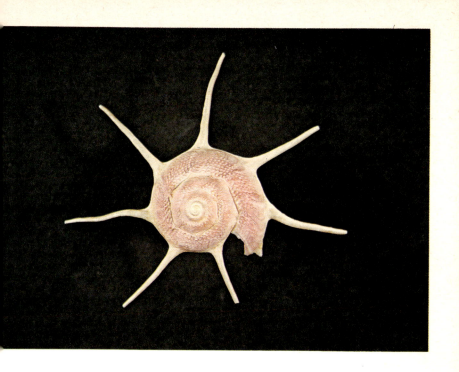

11 *Scientific name* *Guilfordia yoka*

Family Turbinidae

Common name Imperial or Yoca Star-shell

Size 9–12 cm.

Range Japan and Indonesia

The term 'Star-shell' is commonly used for any of the four species of *Guilfordia* or of the many species of the allied genus *Astraea*, where the more numerous spines are much shorter and may be flattened and roughly triangular in shape or may be folded, causing corrugations on the whorls. The best known of the *Guilfordias* is *G. triumphans*, which closely resembles the shell illustrated, but has shorter spines. It is from the same area, but has also been recorded recently from Queensland. Both species are from fairly deep water.

12 *Scientific name* Phasianella australis

Family Phasianellidae

Common name Australian Pheasant Shell or Painted Lady

Size 5–10 cm.

Range Southern Australia, including Tasmania, but not New South Wales

There seems to be no end to the wonderful range of intricate colour patterns which are a feature of this, the largest of the Pheasant Shells. Many of the smaller species are equally colourful. The texture of the shell is like fine glazed porcelain and completely smooth, with no trace of iridescence. There is a solid white operculum. The molluscs live from just below low-water mark down to a depth of about 60 feet, and are said to feed on only one species of sea-weed. Like some of the top shells, they have a peculiar mode of locomotion, advancing first one side of the foot and then the other, while the opposite side remains stationary. Empty shells are often to be found on sandy beaches.

3 *Scientific name*   *Angaria delphinus*
Family   Angariidae
Common name   Fringed Dolphin Shell
Size   5–7 cm.
Range   Indo-Pacific

These are solid, heavy shells, lined with mother-of-pearl, and often decorated on the outside with strange, stumpy outgrowths, which can resemble hands with fingers, and by curving in the direction of growth may impart a strange 'centrifugal' effect. The spire is depressed, or flattened, and the whorls may be distinctly angular in outline when viewed from above, especially in the form *euracantha*, shown on the right. There is a deep umbilicus, and in life the aperture is closed by a brown horny operculum. The species is found on coral reefs at low water.

14 *Scientific name*   *Epitonium scalare*
Family   Epitoniidae
Common name   Precious Wentletrap
Size   5–7 cm.
Range   Indo-Pacific

During the eighteenth century, when few specimens were available, this species was considered by collectors to be one of the most desirable of all shells, and high prices were paid at auctions for large and perfect specimens. The Chinese are said to have taken advantage of this by producing counterfeits made of rice-paste and selling them as the genuine article. It is no longer considered a rare shell, but good specimens are still in demand among collectors.

The flesh-coloured whorls are very loosely coiled, the white ribs being the only point of contact between them. Wentletraps are carnivorous, and can exude a violet fluid when disturbed. The name 'Wentletrap' is a corruption of the German *Wendeltreppe*, meaning a winding staircase.

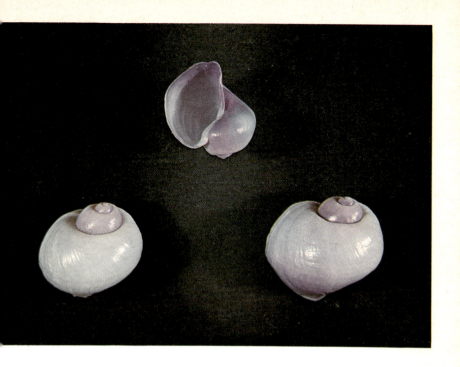

15 *Scientific name* Janthina prolongata
Family Janthinidae
Common name Violet Sea-snail
Size 2·5–3·5 cm.
Range Indo-Pacific

The Violet Sea-snails, of which there are several species, are truly pelagic, enormous colonies of them and of the small jelly-fish on which they feed, drifting with the currents in mid-ocean, and occasionally being blown ashore in such vast numbers that the whole beach seems to take on a violet hue. The shells are extremely fragile, and in both sexes the mollusc creates a raft of mucus which traps air bubbles as it hardens and acts as a float, to one end of which it is attached, aperture upwards. In this species the egg capsules of the female are cemented to the underside of her raft in regular rows, those farthest from the animal hatching first. These sea-snails are totally blind. The coloration of the shell is protective, blending with its surroundings, and, like the Wentletraps, the mollusc can discharge a violet fluid into the water if disturbed. Predators which are a constant threat include both sea-birds and fish.

16 *Scientific name* Carinaria lamarcki
Family Carinariidae
Common name Glassy Nautilus
Size Up to 4·5 cm. (shell)
Range Atlantic and Mediterranean, in warmer waters

The common name for this small group of shells is misleading, for although the transparent shell slightly resembles that of the Paper Nautilus, the animal is not a nautilus, but a gastropod, which lives its whole life swimming upside down near the surface of the sea. In this species the roughly cylindrical animal is about 25 cm. long, the delicate shell, which covers the gills, perched on its back like the saddle on a horse, though because of the inverted position it is actually hanging *below* the creature as it swims by means of a fish-like fin at the hind end. The body, like the shell, is almost transparent.

Another species, *C. cristata* from the Indo-Pacific has a larger though equally fragile shell with a less curved apex, and this was once so highly prized by collectors that it was said to be the rarest of all shells. Few collectors would give much for it now.

7 *Scientific name* Xenophora pallidula

Family Xenophoridae

Common name Japanese Carrier Shell

Size 4–7 cm.

Range Japan to Philippine Is., and South Africa

Carrier shells are so called because many of them, including the present species, attach to their own shells an assortment of other shells, bits of rock or coral and other debris from the sea-bed, these objects being firmly cemented into place one by one at the periphery of the shell during growth. As each whorl overlaps the next one the attached shells remain in position, so that the conical carrier shell is completely hidden from above (specimen on right) or from the side (specimen on left), resulting in a very effective camouflage. Single valves of bivalve shells are always attached with the hollow surface uppermost, so that they do not impede the animal's progress. It moves by pushing its operculum into the sand with its foot and pulling itself along in a series of jerks. The mollusc has been nicknamed 'the Conchologist' because it 'collects' other shells. With these the total diameter may be 10 cm. or more.

18 *Scientific name*   *Stellaria solaris*

Family   Xenophoridae

Common name   Sunburst Carrier Shell

Size   8–10 cm.

Range   Western Pacific

Some carrier shells do not ornament their dwellings by cementing on empty shells or other objects, and some kinds just attach very small bits of stone so that they form a row along the *suture* (the line or groove where two whorls meet), but this particular species obviously feels the need for *some* kind of ornamentation, and produces radiating hollow spines to give a very beautiful effect. Whereas in *Guilfordia* (p. 11) the spines of the preceding whorl are dissolved away when the next whorl overlaps it, in this shell the spines of the earlier whorls remain, forming an attractive ornamentation on the upper part of the succeeding whorls, while the fine beaded cords on the underside curve outwards from the narrow umbilicus, and seem to twist together to decorate the spines. There can be few shells which display such exquisite sculpture.

19 *Scientific name* Architectonica trochlearis

Family Architectonicidae

Common name Pacific Sundial or Winding Staircase Shell

Size 6–7 cm.

Range Pacific Ocean

This is the largest of a small but widespread group of shells which are very similar in general shape but differ in details of colour pattern and sculpture. The chief feature which they have in common is the large umbilicus, its edge bordered by little ribs or beads, resembling a spiral staircase as it winds its way upwards into the very apex of the shell. Sometimes as many as half a dozen baby sundial shells have been found sheltering inside the umbilicus of a living adult shell. There is a horny operculum, and the lining of the shell is not pearly. The animals prefer a sandy bottom in fairly deep water.

20 *Scientific name*   Strombus aratrum

Family   Strombidae

Common name   Black-mouth Stromb

Size   6–9 cm.

Range   North-east Queensland, South Papua and Indonesia

The Strombs, sometimes called Conchs, are of world-wide distribution and are favourites with collectors, there being fifty living species and about twenty sub-species, showing great diversity of form and colour. The lip in adult Strombs is frequently much thickened and expanded and has a 'U'-shaped notch, through which the stalk of the right eye protrudes, at the end of the lip farthest from the apex.

    This beautiful shell, with its very distinctive coloration, is not uncommon between tide-marks on sandy beaches where it occurs. Three other species, *S. aurisdianae*, *S. bulla* and *S. vomer*, much resemble it in shape, but all lack the rich, brownish-orange coloration of the aperture which makes this species so distinctive.

21 *Scientific name* Strombus gallus

Family Strombidae

Common name Rooster-tail or Angel Wing Conch

Size 10–15 cm.

Range West Indies to Brazil, rarely in South-east Florida

Somewhat similar in form to the Black-mouth Stromb, with the same flaring lip ending in a stout spike, though here it projects well beyond the tip of the spire. The Strombs are scavengers, feeding on carrion, or vegetarians. They are extremely active and use the same method of progression as the Carrier Shells (see p. 17) moving in a series of leaps. This species is rather rare, though many species are abundant in the vicinity of coral reefs.

22 *Scientific name* Strombus sinuatus

Family Strombidae

Common name Laciniated Conch

Size 8–12 cm.

Range South-west Pacific

The chief beauty of this lovely shell lies in the deep brownish-purple aperture and in the thin, scalloped hind edge of the lip, which extends in an arc from the tip of the spire to the thickened mid-portion of the lip, terminating in a deep notch at the base. It occurs from low-tide mark to a depth of about 60 feet in areas of coral sand, and may occur in considerable numbers in some places especially on offshore islands. There are only a few records from northern Australia.

23 *Scientific name* Strombus listeri

Family Strombidae

Common name Lister's Conch

Size 10–15 cm.

Range Arabian Sea and Bay of Bengal

Although first described in 1852, only five further examples of the adult shell of this species came to light in the next 100 years, and in 1966 it was said that there might still be less than a dozen specimens in collections. Since then, as a result of trawling, many more have been found, but fine specimens are still much in demand, for it is a shell of surpassing elegance and a prize for any collector. It comes from deep water, the specimen illustrated having been trawled in about 270 feet on a silt and sand bottom off western Thailand.

24 *Scientific name* Strombus gigas
Family Strombidae
Common name Queen Conch
Size Up to 30 cm.
Range West Indies, Bermuda and South-east Florida

This is probably one of the most familiar shells, its large size and beautiful pink interior making it a favourite with flower-arrangers, while the animal is much esteemed for food, being eaten as chowder and as conch steak. It is abundant on the sand flats in shallow water which are its home. Pink pearls are sometimes obtained from it. The shell was formerly used as a trumpet on southern plantations, and has also been made use of for cutting cameos, though it is not ideal for the purpose. The outside of the shell is covered by a brownish horny periostracum, which flakes off when dry.

Scientific name Lambis digitata

Family Strombidae

Common name Elongate Spider Conch

Size 12–14 cm.

Range Indian and Western Pacific Oceans

Often known as scorpion shells, or spider conchs, most members of this genus differ from the true Strombs in having stout curved spines protruding from the outer edge of the lip of the adult shell. These are not present in juvenile shells, which can cause problems in identification because they look so different. In some species, of which this is one, the spines are quite short. The narrow slit-like aperture in most *Lambis* is bordered with conspicuous fine ridges, there being two exceptions where the borders are smooth. This species is rather rare.

26 *Scientific name* Lambis violacea
Family Strombidae
Common name Violet Spider Conch
Size 7–12 cm.
Range Indian Ocean; most specimens from Mauritius

This is the rarest of the spider conchs, although not perhaps as rare as one might suppose after reading a statement made in 1961 that there were possibly not more than 100 known specimens. One was sold by auction in London for £5 in 1971, and another for £3 in 1972. It is certainly a most beautiful shell, with the white aperture setting off the violet interior, the large orange spots on the lip and the narrow bands with chevron markings on the columella. All the spider conchs are vegetarians, at least one species feeding almost exclusively on fine red algae.

27 *Scientific name* Tibia fusus

Family Strombidae

Common name Spindle or Shinbone Tibia

Size Up to 32 cm.

Range Western Pacific, especially Philippine Is.

A fine specimen of this shell can hardly fail to evoke a gasp of admiration from someone seeing it for the first time. The tall spire and tremendously long and slender siphonal canal, the rich coloration and the five 'fingers' or short spines on the outer lip, the top of which ends in a little 'scroll', as if to put the finishing touch to this masterpiece of design – all add up to a shell which has most of the qualities a collector could wish for. It is found at depths down to 130 feet. There is a form *melanocheilus* where the lip is stained with blackish-purple. Only half a dozen species of *Tibia* are known, and all are considered uncommon or rare.

28 *Scientific name* Terebellum terebellum

Family Strombidae

Common name Little Screw Shell

Size 4–6 cm.

Range Indian and Western Pacific Oceans and Red Sea

Only a single species of *Terebellum* is known, although there are a number of distinct colour patterns, the three most usual, shown above, being (from left to right) forma *punctulorum*, forma *nebulosum* and forma *lineatum*.

The animal of this moderately common species is very active, living in sandy areas in shallow water and burrowing horizontally just below the surface of the sand. As it progresses it first pushes one eye up to the surface like a periscope and moves forward, the eye remaining stationary until the elastic eye-stalk is stretched to its fullest extent. The second eye is then pushed above the surface and the first one retracted, the body continuing to move forward at a fairly steady rate, while the process is repeated again and again, each eye in turn surveying the terrain.

9 *Scientific name* Ovulum ovum

Family Ovulidae

Common name Egg Shell or Poached Egg Cowry

Size 4·5–10 cm.

Range Indo-Pacific

More than almost any other shell in the Indo-Pacific area, this abundant and very striking shell has been used by man in a variety of ways – to decorate his houses and his canoes, to adorn his person and above all as a fertility charm, its reputed magical properties even extending to his crops. Pure white outside, the inside of the shell varies in colour in different specimens, from a deep chocolate-brown to a brick red. The animal is jet black, the colour relieved by small white *papillae* or filamentous outgrowths from the surface of the mantle.

30 *Scientific name*   Volva volva

Family   Ovulidae

Common name   Spindle Shell or Elongated Egg Cowry

Size   5–10 cm., exceptionally to 16 cm.

Range   Indo–West Pacific, with a subspecies in the Caribbean

The shape of this moderately common shell makes it quite unmistakable, for no other shell of this size has the beak-like terminal projections which give it its name, and which may dissuade predators from attempting to eat it. These beaks may be straight or slightly curved. The colour of the shell varies from a pale cream to a lightish pink. Many of the smaller 'egg cowries' live among the branches of corals, but this species has been noted in areas of fine sand in Japanese waters. The Caribbean form is subsp. *striata*.

31 *Scientific name* Cypraea ocellata

Family Cypraeidae

Common name Ocellated Cowry

Size 2–3 cm.

Range Gulf of Oman to Java, and Andaman Is.

This lovely shell typifies many of the smaller cowries, which appeal to collectors because of their high gloss and beautiful colour schemes: these can vary considerably even within one species, as can be seen above. There are nearly 200 species of true cowries, including many rarities and many which are very common, though this species lies somewhere between the two categories. The gloss is imparted by the two mantle flaps, which when extended cover the shell and meet at the *pallial line*, which shows well in the shell on the left. This line is not always present. The view of the underside, on the right, shows the 'teeth' which border the slit-like aperture in most cowries.

32 *Scientific name* Cypraea tessellata
Family Cypraeidae
Common name Checkerboard Cowry
Size 2–3 cm.
Range Hawaiian chain of islands

For many years specimens of this shell, which appeared infrequently in collections, were dull and bleached beach shells or yellowish sub-fossils. It was not until 1955 that living specimens were obtained in about 30 feet of water by aqualung divers, and their true beauty revealed. They live in or under coral heads, which have to be broken open to reach them, and their rarity and unique appearance make them great favourites with collectors. The aperture of the shell is so narrow that it is difficult to see how the animal can squeeze its body through such a small space. Note the squarish blotches on the side of the shell in the centre, which account for both the specific name and the common name. They are not always so evenly spaced, but may be even more so.

Scientific name Cypraea granulata

Family Cypraeidae

Common name Granulated Cowry

Size 2–4 cm.

Range Hawaiian chain of islands

Most true cowries have a smooth, glossy shell, but in a few the shell is covered with little 'pimples' or *nodules*, and in *this* species every trace of gloss, which is present in young shells, disappears on reaching maturity. Nevertheless, live-collected shells are truly beautiful, especially when examined under a lens, for red lines encircle the nodules and run along the ridges connecting them, while on the base, which is covered with transverse ridges, these are thrown into sharp relief by the red lines which border them. The mantle of the animal is decorated with long, branched, green-tipped papillae, and, like the previous species, the mollusc lives under or in coral heads and slabs, where it was inaccessible until the development of the aqualung in about 1953. It may be found in shallow and in quite deep water.

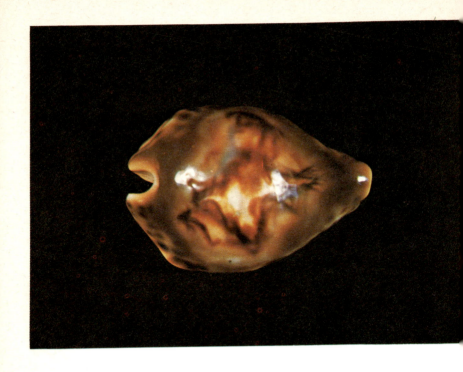

34 *Scientific name*   Cypraea fultoni

Family   Cypraeidae

Common name   Fulton's Cowry

Size   5–6·5 cm.

Range   Deep water off South Africa, especially Natal

Some of the rarest deep-water shells, of which this is one, are almost always recovered from the stomachs of fish, particularly *Sparodon durbanensis*, the 'Musselcracker'. Unless removed within a few hours of having been swallowed, the stomach acids will ruin them, even if they have not already been damaged by the fish's teeth, as often happens. No one has yet located the exact habitat of this cowry, or seen the living animal, and the total number of specimens in collections may be less than two dozen. The very angular outline is characteristic. An allied but smaller and shallow-water species, *C. teulerei*, was considered equally rare until 1970, when it was found in quantity on Masira Island, off the coast of Oman.

In Florida, no fewer than 425 species of shells have been taken from the stomach and intestines of the Bat Fish, a bottom feeder.

(Shell from the J. D. Orr collection)

35 *Scientific name* Cypraea friendii

Family Cypraeidae

Common name Friend's Cowry

Size 7–9 cm.

Range South-west and South Australia

The name *friendii* was formerly restricted to the rather narrow, boat-shaped shells of the typical form from South-west Australia, which are found feeding on orange sponges attached to piles in harbours, or in much greater depths, where the sponges are growing on weed-covered flats. The shells are light in weight, with rather fragile upturned ends and often with a certain amount of blue coloration, particularly in younger shells, which enhances their beauty. It is now felt that other, heavier and more 'swollen' shells which were formerly thought to be species, under such names as *vercoi, contraria* (a very pale shell) and *thersites* (from South Australia), should all be included in this very variable species.

36 *Scientific name*   *Cypraea aurantium*
Family   Cypraeidae
Common name   Golden Cowry
Size   8–13 cm.
Range   Central and West Pacific

What this splendid shell lacks by way of pattern it more than makes up for by its coloration, which in freshly collected shells may vary from a deep magenta to a rich golden-orange hue, the margins and underside being creamy white, with orange 'teeth' bordering the aperture. Some older shells are found to be perforated on one side, having been suspended on a cord or attached to clothing and worn in Fiji and other Pacific islands as a symbol of authority. There is an insatiable demand among collectors for this shell and prices remain high, although in 1970 some 300 specimens were known in collections, and many more will have been collected since then.

    The animals are equally striking, the dark grey mantle besprinkled with white dots bearing two sorts of cream-coloured papillae, many of them branched. These molluscs live in caves, on the windward side of reefs, at various depths down to 60 feet and more, and are nocturnal feeders, browsing on algae.

Scientific name Cypraea argus
Family Cypraeidae
Common name Eyed Cowry
Size 6–9 cm.
Range Indo-Pacific

The distinctive colour pattern of brown rings or 'eyes' on a fawn background makes this one of the easiest cowries to identify, but it also poses problems. By what mechanism does the mantle-edge produce such a pattern? Are the pigment-producing cells also in circles? If so, how can the pattern be formed so distinctly when the mantle is constantly moving over the surface? In immature shells only the broad transverse bands are present; the rings are superimposed on them later. The dark blotches on the base are a consistent feature. The species is moderately common in some places.

   The purchase of one of these shells by the author, while still a schoolboy may have been responsible for his lifelong interest in conchology, culminating in the writing of this book.

38 *Scientific name* Cypraea mappa

Family Cypraeidae

Common name Map Cowry

Size 5–8 cm.

Range Indo-Pacific

The intricate pattern which distinguishes this handsome cowry from all others is laid down in two final stages, one set of fine lines being superimposed on the other. The wide 'pallial line' (see *Cypraea ocellata*, p. 31), devoid of any markings, is one of the most conspicuous features and is quite unique, for short, spoon-shaped branches lead off from it in an irregular manner on either side. The resulting pattern bears a fanciful resemblance to a map – hence the name. The base may be creamy, or suffused with pink or bright violet, while the 'teeth' which border the aperture are orange.

Though widely distributed, it is not a common shell, and it is a great favourite with collectors. There is a rare form (forma *panerythra*) where the whole shell is suffused with a deep pinkish hue.

39 *Scientific name* Cypraea reevei

Family Cypraeidae

Common name Reeve's Cowry

Size About 3·5 cm.

Range South Australia to Western Australia

As is the case with the Golden Cowry, the beauty of this shell lies not in any complex pattern, but in the effect of the combination of two colours – in the present instance the grey or sometimes fawn colour of the body whorl and the deep pink of the two extremities. The base is almost white. Many cowry collectors have not seen this shell in good condition, for good specimens are rare. Unlike most cowries, the glossy surface of the shell is uneven, having shallow pits which give it the appearance of beaten metal, the term used to describe it being 'malleated'. It is thin, and light in weight, and quite variable in shape, almost spherical forms sometimes being found in deep water, though the species also occurs in the intertidal zone.

40 *Scientific name*   Tonna perdix
Family   Tonnidae
Common name   Partridge Shell
Size   5–15 cm., exceptionally to 19 cm.
Range   Indo-Pacific

This shell and its allies are known collectively as Tun Shells, from their alleged similarity in shape to casks of wine. They are a small group with few species, and all have a thin shell with a very large and swollen body whorl, the surface being covered with flat ribs. The white grooves between these ribs and the crescent-shaped markings which connect them make this species the most handsome of the group. The animal is considerably larger than the shell. It is fairly common, inhabiting weed-covered flats on the outer edge of coral reefs.

There is a very similar species, *T. maculosa*, in the Caribbean.

1 *Scientific name* Cypraecassis rufa
Family Cassidae
Common name Bull Mouth or Red Helmet Shell
Size 6·5–20 cm.
Range Indo-Pacific

This is the shell which has been used, perhaps, more than any other for the production of cameos since shells were first used for this purpose about 150 years ago. Large quantities are still exported from East Africa, where it is abundant, to Italy, where most of the cameos are made. It is also a common shell in Polynesia, though quite rare in the intervening western Pacific.

The roughly egg-shaped, reddish-brown shell bears three or four rows of rounded knobs, which are replaced by numerous cream-coloured ribs as it tapers towards the front end, but the real beauty lies in the *base* of the shell, which is shown above. Helmet shells live in shallow water near coral reefs, and feed on spiny sea-urchins. They are among the largest and heaviest gastropods, some of the sixty odd species attaining a length of nearly 40 cm.

42 *Scientific name*   *Charonia tritonis*
Family   Cymatiidae
Common name   Triton's Trumpet
Size   15–45 cm.
Range   Indo-Pacific

One of the largest, most colourful and best-known shells, this species is widely distributed over the Indo-Pacific region, sometimes being found in shallow water, but seeming to prefer rather deeper waters, where it can shelter in caves or under ledges. The egg capsules of this species are club-shaped, about 2 to 3 cm. long, and laid in large clusters. There are about a dozen species, with a world-wide distribution. They all have a horny operculum.

   Islanders in the Pacific have for generations used this shell as a cooking utensil and also, as the name suggests, as a trumpet, a hole being drilled near the apex of the spire into which a mouthpiece was sometimes inserted. The low-pitched booming note has been likened to that of a foghorn.
(Shell from the W. Karo collection)

Scientific name Biplex perca
Family Bursidae
Common name Winged Frog Shell
Size 4–7 cm.
Range Western Pacific

There are about sixty species of Frog Shells, which vary considerably in shape. Most of these are included in the genus *Bursa*, but a smaller number are placed under *Biplex*, and of these only three species have this characteristic shape, with these beautiful ribbed, wing-like processes fanning out on either side. One of these, *B. jucundum*, is much smaller and is commonly known in Queensland as the 'Cockaroo' or 'Kookaburra Shell', from the great resemblance to a bird's head when held in the left hand by the apex with the aperture towards one, in the position shown on the left, above. Neither species is particularly rare.

44 *Scientific name*   *Bursa candisata*

Family   Bursidae

Common name   Candied Frog Shell

Size   10–12·5 cm.

Range   Western Pacific

The specific name of this rather unusual Frog Shell is quite appropriate, for it is so thickly covered with rows of little granules that it does indeed almost appear to be coated with sugar. Some of the smaller granules are so regular that they appear like strings of tiny pearls. The shell demonstrates another feature of most, though not all, Frog Shells. This is that there are only two varices (see Introduction, p. xviii) to each whorl. In the present species these take the form of corrugated ribs, which are slightly staggered instead of being exactly in line. The shape is much more elongated than in most Frog Shells, which are normally rather squat.

45 *Scientific name* Murex tribulus

Family Muricidae

Common name Bramble Murex

Size 7–12 cm.

Range Indian and Western Pacific Oceans

In this enormous and very variable family there are about a dozen species having this very long siphonal canal and these long, slender spines. They are sometimes referred to as 'typical Murex' or even just 'spiny Murex', though this is rather a vague term and could lead to confusion. The spines are certainly a defence mechanism, and in fine examples of the Bramble Murex one particular spine always far exceeds the others. It is a fairly common shell, though not often seen in such perfect condition.

An allied species, the Venus's Comb Shell, *M. pecten*, has on each of its three varices a row of long spines set closely together, those on the canal being even longer and curving at the tips. Though the species is not rare, perfect specimens with intact spines have been prized by collectors since the very early days.

(Shell from the A. P. H. Oliver collection)

46 *Scientific name* Murex (Bolinus) cornutus
Family Muricidae
Common name Horned Murex
Size About 15 cm.
Range West Africa

Some *Murex* species, of which this is a good example, build a shell where the spines on the shoulder, or widest part of the spire, curve in an anti-clockwise direction when viewed from the apex, giving the same beautiful 'centrifugal' effect which is so noticeable in the dolphin shells (p. 13). Here the effect is emphasized, because the base of the hollow spine splits, half of it being continued across the spire as a strong corrugated rib, these ribs forming a delightful pattern in bold relief (see shell on the right).

The animal of a closely related and common Mediterranean species, *M. brandaris*, which has a smaller shell with short, straight spines, was one of the chief sources of the dye 'Tyrian purple', monopolized for their robes by the ruling classes in Ancient Rome.

Scientific name   Murex (Pterynotus) alatus

Family   Muricidae

Common name   Pinnate Murex

Size   6–8 cm.

Range   Indian and Western Pacific Oceans

Perhaps better known under the name *M. pinnatus*, to which it may yet revert, this normally pure white shell is deservedly popular with collectors, for it is a very lovely species. Some *Murex* have spines, some have knobs, but those placed in the sub-genus *Pterynotus* have three fin-like varices which in this species have a slight spiral twist instead of being in a straight line. Delicate transverse ribs accentuate the contours, and the absence of colour only increases one's appreciation of such beauty. Though widely distributed, it is nowhere very common, and therefore all the more desirable.

48 *Scientific name* Murex (Chicoreus) palmarosae

Family Muricidae

Common name Rose-branch Murex

Size 8–12 cm.

Range Indian and Western Pacific Oceans

With its rose-tipped branching fronds taking the place of spines on the three varices, this well-known shell illustrates yet again the amazing versatility displayed by these molluscs. One can speculate as to whether this elaborate ornamentation is a sort of camouflage or whether it is formed for some other reason, but one of the side-effects is certainly to give pleasure to all shell-lovers. The overall effect is so bizarre that people have likened the shell to some strange prehistoric monster.

49 *Scientific name*   *Murex (Chicoreus) cervicornis*

Family   Muricidae

Common name   Stag's-horn or Two-forked Murex

Size   3–6 cm.

Range   South-west Pacific

This rather fragile-looking shell is easily recognized by the largest spines being forked, like a deer's antlers: these spines often become encrusted with various marine growths. The specimen illustrated is interesting historically, being one of a large number which were collected in the Arafura Sea, north of Australia, in 1881 by Staff-Surgeon R. W. Coppinger, R.N., during the cruise of H.M.S. *Alert*. Many of these shells still had the original parchment labels tied to them with thread, giving full details of place, depth, etc., from which they were collected – a valuable record. The species can occur at considerable depths, down to 600 feet, and the colour of the shell varies from white to fawn, or even occasionally a deep brown hue.

    A much larger Australian species, *M. cornucervi*, with big, curving spines, is also sometimes called the Stag's-horn Murex, which is rather confusing unless one knows about it.

50 *Scientific name* Murex (Ceratostoma) burnetti

Family Muricidae

Common name Burnett's Murex

Size 9–12 cm.

Range Pacific Ocean

In some specimens of this little-known but very handsome *Murex* the conspicuous ribbed or folded varices are pale in colour, in marked contrast to the rich brown body whorl. In others, both varices and body whorl are uniformly brown. A distinctive feature is the presence of a single 'tooth' on the outer edge of the aperture, which remains projecting in the direction of growth from successive varices as growth continues. It is conjectured that this 'tooth', which is present in a few other gastropod shells, may be used to wedge open the valves of bivalve shells while it feeds on the soft tissues of the animals within.

This species has been reported from such widely scattered localities as Sitka, Alaska, Japan, Taiwan and north-west Australia, but its exact distribution is not known.

(Shell from the W. Karo collection)

51 *Scientific name* Murex (Hexaplex) cichoreus

Family Muricidae

Common name Endive Murex

Size 5–10 cm.

Range Indo-Pacific, excluding Australia

The short curved and frilled spines, which give this shell its common name, are nearly always dark brown in colour, though the rest of the shell may be pure white, or may have brown streaks running back from the spines or may be conspicuously banded with brown. A thin pink line often encircles the aperture, and in some specimens there is a deep umbilicus. The species is not a rare one, and many specimens come from the Philippines, the home of so many fine shells.

A most attractive variety from the same area, var. *saxicola*, shown on the right, with a broadly conical instead of a 'stepped' spire, and more numerous varices, is particularly lovely.

52 *Scientific name* Murex (Homalocantha) scorpio

Family Muricidae

Common name Scorpion Murex

Size 2·5–6 cm.

Range South-west Pacific

This is a shell of singularly grotesque appearance, with its four or five T-shaped spines projecting from the outer lip of the aperture and joined by web-like sculpture at the base, its long siphonal canal and the upper or posterior whorls almost separated from the final whorl by a deep suture. The colour varies from white through various shades of brown to almost black. It is quite uncommon, and little is known about the animal or its habits. As the shell increases in size the animal dissolves the earlier spines by chemical action.

Allied Pacific species include *M. rota* (*M. anatomica* and the Hawaiian *M. pele* are probably variants of this species), *M. zamboi* and *M. secunda*.

53 *Scientific name* Trophon (Austrotrophon) catalinensis
Family Muricidae
Common name Three-cornered or Catalina Trophon
Size 5–10 cm.
Range Deep water off Southern California

The elegant lines of this uncommon shell, with its very thin, overlapping, wing-like varices giving it a triangular outline, make it one of the most sought-after shells on the Pacific coast of America where shell-collectors are concerned. At the shoulder these varices are produced as hollow spines, extending almost to a level with or even beyond the apex. It is a pleasing light-brown colour, with longitudinal darker streaks faintly visible, and a white aperture.

54 *Scientific name*   Trophon geversianum

Family   Muricidae

Common name   Magellanic Trophon

Size   5–7 cm.

Range   Patagonia and Falkland Islands

This is among the largest of the *Trophons*, a group which inhabit colder waters than *Murex*, and often at considerable depths. The animal is carnivorous, feeding on mussels. Like many cold-water shells, there is an almost total absence of colour, apart from the brown interior, but the exquisite sculpture, consisting of longitudinal wafer-thin varices intersected by transverse ribs, more than compensates for this. The shell is quite light and fragile. Most specimens collected are beach-worn, and in these the varices hardly rise above the surface and the shell loses much of its beauty.

Other *Trophon* species seldom exceed 2 cm. in length, but some are very lovely, and also very rare.

Scientific name   Latiaxis mawae

Family   Magilidae

Common name   Mawe's Latiaxis

Size   4–5 cm.

Range   Western Pacific from Japan to Australia

Like the Trophons, the members of the small genus Latiaxis are from deep water and are almost devoid of colour, but are prized by collectors for their rarity and for the many beautiful variations in shell sculpture which they exhibit. This species, the largest of the genus, has a perfectly flat spire, but the body whorl, with its row of incurving triangular spines at the shoulder, descends very steeply, and seems as if it is trying to unwind itself from the columella. This is hollow, and expands into a large, funnel-shaped umbilicus with a serrated edge. A horny operculum, conspicuous in the above specimen, closes the aperture, and there is a curving, open-sided siphonal canal. The net result is one of the strangest-looking shells one could imagine.

56 *Scientific name* Latiaxis tosanus

Family Magilidae

Common name Tosa Bay Latiaxis

Size 2–3 cm.

Range Deep water off Japan

Having pale pink spines on a creamy-white shell and an apex of a rather deeper pink, this must surely be one of the loveliest of the *Latiaxis*. When viewed from the apex (left-hand illustration) the spines radiate from the centre like the petals of a flower. The diameter of the shell slightly exceeds its length, and the short spines below the shoulder, which are not pink like the others, are crowded together in about four rows. The delicacy of the colours matches the delicacy of the shell – a truly beautiful combination. It is in the uncommon to rare category.

57 Scientific name *Latiaxis lischkeana*

Family Magilidae

Common name Lischke's Latiaxis

Size 3–4 cm.

Range Deep water off Japan

Many Japanese shells have this type of spire, which may have been the source of inspiration for their pagodas and similar architectural features, but there can be few with such intricate sculpture, which can only be appreciated fully by examining it with a lens. The angular shoulders of the whorls are embellished with a fringe of flattened, hollow spines which stand out conspicuously, while the rest of the pure white shell is completely covered by row after row of *very minute* spines, reminiscent of the teeth on a fine fretsaw blade, except that they, like the other spines, are pure white and hollow. Subspecies occur in Australia and New Zealand.

Rather more common is *L. japonicus*, which is similar, but with the larger spines more prominent on the upper whorls of the spire, and with the minute spines reduced to overlapping scales on the numerous encircling ridges.

58 Scientific name   Busycon contrarium
Family   Buccinidae
Common name   Lightning Whelk
Size   10–40 cm.
Range   South-east United States

An interesting shell because it is normally sinistral, or 'left-handed', in its manner of coiling (see Introduction, p. xviii), whereas *most* marine shells coil in the reverse direction. Right-handed examples of this species are occasionally found. The egg capsules are joined together in long chains, which are frequently carried in by the tide and left stranded on the beach. There is a large, horny operculum. The Lightning Whelk, so called from the dark streaks which traverse its surface, is quite common and is one of a small genus of shells known as 'Fulgur Whelks', a primitive group which abounded in the oceans in far-off geological times.

Scientific name Melongena corona

Family Buccinidae

Common name Common Crown Conch

Size 4–10 cm.

Range South-east United States and Mexico

So different are the numerous local forms of this variable shell that it is difficult to believe that they are the same species. Some are narrow shells with a great number of spines crowded together at the shoulder and none at the base of the shell, the colour being purplish-brown with narrow white bands. Others may be broad shells with fewer and stouter spines at the shoulder, a row of spines at the base and the colours reversed. The reason for these differences is that all the growth stages are passed within the egg capsule, the young emerging as small adults, only capable of crawling limited distances. The different populations therefore remain isolated, and over a long period develop their own local characteristics.

The animals are carnivorous, many feeding on clams and other bivalves. There is a horny operculum to close the aperture.

60 *Scientific name* Voluta ebraea

Family Volutidae

Common name Hebrew Volute

Size 10–15 cm., but can be much larger

Range North and North-east Brazil

Volutes are often considered by collectors to be the 'aristocrats' of shells, and certainly they are among the most popular groups because of their rich variety of colour patterns, their diverse and attractive shapes and the large number of species (about 200), some of which are very rare. The animals also have very striking colour patterns; often these are totally different from those of the shells. Some volutes, this being one, have a rather small, horny operculum.

An unusual feature of this moderately common species is that the females produce a broad shell, as in the above illustration, while the shell of the male is smaller and much narrower, with less prominent knobs. The common name refers to the supposed resemblance of the pattern to Hebrew script.

61 *Scientific name* Lyria kurodai

Family Volutidae

Common name Kuroda's Volute

Size 6–9 cm.

Range South China Sea, off Taiwan

Many volutes have a completely smooth shell. Others, like the present rare species, have a shell the surface of which is completely covered by ribs set closely together. This species was first described as recently as 1964, and specimens are obtained by trawling in deep water, sometimes at depths of nearly 2,000 feet, which probably explains why, like so many other exciting shells discovered recently, it was not found earlier. It may prove to be not uncommon at such depths, but it is likely to be always in demand.

(Shell from the W. Karo collection)

62 *Scientific name*   Lyria lyraeformis
Family   Volutidae
Common name   Lyre Volute
Size   8–14·5 cm.
Range   Off the coast of Kenya

This lovely volute embodies most of the features which collectors consider to be the qualities of a desirable shell. It has a slender, graceful shape accentuated by the closely set ribs; a delightful colour pattern, the colour sometimes approaching dark green in freshly collected specimens, but more usually various shades of brown and chestnut on a fawn background; and also the attraction of being quite rare.

Fossil evidence shows that shells very similar to the various species of *Lyria* existed in remote geological times.

3 *Scientific name* Cymbiola cymbiola
Family Volutidae
Common name None
Size 6–8·5 cm.
Range Indonesia

Few examples of this rare shell are known outside museums, and as far as is known not a single specimen, alive or dead, has been collected within living memory. This does not mean that the species is extinct. The locality 'Moluccas' given on labels in museums may be too imprecise or may even be incorrect, and, as with other rare shells, there may be a thriving population in some remote spot which may be located when some interested person stumbles across it. This has happened with a number of rare species in the last few years. It is this exciting possibility which makes shell-collecting such a fascinating hobby.

Even as this book goes to press, there is a report that shells resembling this species have been trawled by Taiwan fishermen off the north coast of Australia.

64 *Scientific name* Cymbiola (Aulica) imperialis

Family Volutidae

Common name Imperial Volute

Size 10–25 cm.

Range Southern Philippine Is.

This is well named the Imperial Volute, for it is a shell of massive proportions, yet with an air of distinction imparted by the 'crown' of hollow spines at the shoulder and the smaller ones on the spire. There are four strong folds or plaits on the columella, and the colour of the aperture varies from cream to orange. In 1786 a particularly fine specimen was sold by auction for £24 3s., but by 1822 another fine specimen was sold for only £8 15s., and today specimens could possibly be obtained for half that price. There is a colour form which has been called *robinsona*: it lacks the broad chestnut bands of the typical shell. The species occurs at various depths, from shallow water down to 60 feet, usually on a sandy bottom.

65 *Scientific name* Cymbiola (Aulicina) nivosa

Family Volutidae

Common name Snowy Volute

Size 6–8·5 cm.

Range North-west Australia

Flecked with white all over, except for the striped portion above the shoulder and the two patterned bands which encircle the body whorl, it is easy to see why the typical narrow form of this handsome shell was called the Snowy Volute. The dark blue-grey colour of fresh shells fades to a pinkish colour as they age. The columella is pale brownish orange with four plaits, and the aperture grey-brown.

There is a broader form of this shell (right-hand specimen) with spines at the shoulder, more diffuse markings and grey-green and pale orange the predominating colours. It is so different in appearance that it was once thought to be a distinct species, and is sometimes referred to under the name *oblita*. Both forms are fairly common.

66 *Scientific name* Harpulina arausiaca
Family Volutidae
Common name Flag Volute
Size 6·5–8·5 cm.
Range Northern Ceylon and southern India

Known to collectors in the eighteenth century as the 'Prince of Orange's Flag Volute', or more simply the 'Orange Flag Volute', this shell has always been valued because of its remarkable colour pattern, reminiscent of the stripes on a flag and laid down with great regularity. It is still rather a rare shell, and has been recorded at a depth of about 70 feet in areas where the sea-bed is sandy.

Scientific name   *Volutoconus bednalli*
Family   Volutidae
Common name   Bednall's Volute
Size   9–13 cm.
Range   Arafura Sea, North Australia, Papua, south-east Indonesia

Perhaps the most striking of all the volutes, with its distinctive and unique colour pattern, this shell was once so rare as to be almost unobtainable, but of recent years more and more specimens have been obtained off northern Australia by Japanese pearl fishermen. As the demand always exceeds the supply prices remain high and the incentive to collect further shells remains. It is when dredging or trawling for shells on a *commercial* scale occurs, in the hope of making a large profit, that shell-lovers have real cause for concern.

The animal prefers sandy areas at depths of from about 30 to 300 feet.

68 *Scientific name*   *Volutoconus grossi*

Family   Volutidae

Common name   Gross' Volute

Size   7–12 cm.

Range   Off southern Queensland and northern N.S.W.

First described less than fifty years ago, this species is as distinctive in its own way as Bednall's Volute, but the typical form lives at greater depths, down to 600 feet. The shell has the appearance of having been 'squeezed' into a narrow shape, the whorls of the spire having been slightly distorted in the process, so that they do not sit squarely on each other, the turns of the suture not being parallel.

    A very beautiful subspecies, *mcmichaeli*, was described in 1966. It occurs further north, in shallower waters near Townsville, and is smaller and slimmer, with interrupted black bands, and with fine ribs on the upper portion of the spire. Both shells are illustrated for comparison.

69 *Scientific name* Scaphella (Scaphella) junonia

Family Volutidae

Common name The Junonia

Size 8–14 cm.

Range North Carolina to Alabama and Yucatan, Mexico

Rarely picked up on the beaches, and therefore long regarded as a great prize by collectors, the Junonia is nevertheless tolerably plentiful at depths of from 50 to 250 feet, often being brought in by fishermen. The typical form has a creamy background, but off Alabama shells have a brownish-yellow tinge (forma *johnstonae*), while off Yucatan the background is white, with smaller spots (forma *butleri*). The association of the goddess Juno with peacocks presumably led the great nineteenth-century collector and author, Reeve, to coin the name 'Peacock Tail Volute' for this shell, the spots being distributed evenly like the 'eyes' on the peacock's tail.

The animal is said to resemble the shell in coloration, though with larger spots.

70 *Scientific name* Scaphella (Aurinia) dubia
Family Volutidae
Common name Dubious Volute
Size 5·5–22·5 cm.
Range North Carolina to Florida and Gulf of Mexico

Now known to be a very large and rather fragile form of *dubia*, an extremely variable species, the form illustrated was until recently described as a different species under the name *kieneri* (Kiener's Volute). It is from deep water, being fairly common at depths of 100 to 300 feet, and good specimens are sometimes brought in by shrimp boats. The lovely lines and regular colour pattern of this graceful shell can hardly fail to excite admiration.

Other 'species' now included under *dubia* are *georgiana* and *schmitti*. Some name-changes are inevitable as our knowledge increases, and collectors should try to adopt a tolerant attitude to them and not use outdated and obsolete names.

1 *Scientific name*   Amoria (Amorena) undulata

Family   Volutidae

Common name   Wavy Volute

Size   7–10 cm.

Range   Southern coasts of Australia, including Tasmania

The pattern of wavy lines which gives this rather common shell its name is very distinctive, and although other volutes *do* have wavy lines, it is unlikely that they would be confused with this species. It may be found at any depth, from the tidal zone down to about 1,500 feet. It is a variable shell, the ground colour varying from cream to burnt orange, and the shape also varying to some extent.

    The animal is said to be cream-coloured with a network of reddish lines superimposed. Amateur collectors can do good work by making careful notes on their observations of living molluscs: far too little is known about them. Shell magazines with big circulations are the ideal medium for disseminating such knowledge.

72 *Scientific name*   *Mitra papalis*
Family   Mitridae
Common name   Papal Mitre
Size   Up to 15 cm.
Range   Indo-Pacific

This is perhaps not quite as common as the well-known Bishop's Mitre, but it is much more handsome, the more numerous spots being dark brownish-red instead of yellow or orange, and the coronations at the shoulder of each whorl being very prominent. There is a cream-coloured aperture with a row of 'teeth' along the outer lip, and four strong ridges on the columella.

  The animal lives in sand at depth of from 20 to 150 feet below the surface of the sea. It has a long proboscis, which is said to enable it to feed on sea-worms in their tubes on the sea bed. If disturbed, it will, like many other mitres, emit a purple dye which stains anything it touches, and which contains a scented substance thought to attract the opposite sex.

73 *Scientific name*   Vexillum regina

Family   Mitridae*

Common name   Queen Mitre

Size   5–7 cm.

Range   Andaman Is. to Moluccas

One of the loveliest shells in a family which contains well over 500 species, the Queen Mitre combines beauty of line and sculptural detail with colouring which sets it off to perfection. The whorls of the ribbed spire rise in steps, the straight sides of the whorls being pure white, encircled in the middle by a hair-line of reddish brown, while a rather broader rich brown line separates the sides from the sloping orange-yellow or sometimes blackish shoulders. The body whorl has an additional band of orange-yellow bordered by blackish lines, while the base of the shell and the tip of the spire are chocolate brown.

   The conventional way of studying such a shell is to have the spire pointing upwards (or towards the top of the page in a book), but one should remember that when the animal moves the shell is more or less horizontal, with the apex of the spire at the *back* and the *base* of the shell, from which the head emerges, at the front.

* See footnote on next page.

74 *Scientific name*   *Vexillum sanguisugum*

Family   Mitridae*

Common name   Blood-sucker or Branded Mitre

Size   3–6 cm.

Range   Indo–West Pacific

Also labelled *V. stigmataria* in some older books, this beautiful species has numerous longitudinal cream-coloured ribs, which are intersected at right angles by closely-set grooves encircling the whorls and giving the ribs a beaded effect. The background colour between the ribs varies from a uniform creamy-white in some shells to a dark grey in others, but the most striking feature is the narrow band of scarlet on each whorl, formed by two beads of each rib being so coloured, like the twin red marks left by a vampire bat. There are two such bands on the body whorl. On younger shells the squarish red dots are single instead of in pairs. The base of the shell and the tip of the spire are chocolate brown.

This is a fairly common species in some areas. Two colour forms are illustrated.

* Some modern authorities consider that members of the genus Vexillum and of the allied genus Pusia should be separated from the Mitridae and placed in a separate family, Vexillidae.

Scientific name   *Afrivoluta pringlei*

Family   Marginellidae

Common name   Pringle's False Volute

Size   8–10 cm.

Range   Deep water off Natal, South Africa

First described in 1947, this interesting shell was for years regarded as being a volute, but in 1963 it was shown that in fact it is closely allied to the *Marginellas*, a large family of about 600 species, popular with collectors, but mostly *small* shells, the majority not exceeding 3 cm. in length. As in the cowries, the mantle can envelop the outside of the shell, imparting a high gloss. Some have very beautiful patterns. There are four ridges or folds on the columella, and in this species these are particularly prominent, with thickened edges. The queer blister-like swelling or callosity at the shoulder, near the top end of the aperture, is a striking and unexplained feature of this rather rare shell.

Most good specimens are dredged from depths of between 350 and 900 feet.

76 *Scientific name* Oliva porphyria

Family Olividae

Common name Tent Olive

Size 6–12 cm.

Range Gulf of California to Panama and the Galapagos Is.

The olive shells, of which there are over fifty species, have always been popular with collectors, their smooth, glossy and very solid shells exhibiting a wide variety of patterns, and some species having many colour forms, which can be rather confusing. The pattern here reminds one of a large encampment of tents of various sizes. Although the pattern varies in detail in individual specimens, the colour remains very constant. This is the largest of all the olives, and certainly one of the most handsome. One feature which is peculiar to this species is that the edge of the outer lip is slightly concave in outline. It is fairly common, and was one of the species brought back to Europe from the New World by the early explorers.

77 *Scientific name* Oliva reticulata

Family Olividae

Common name Blood Olive

Size 3·5–5 cm.

Range Indo–West Pacific

Known formerly as *O. sanguinolenta*, the chief beauty of this shell, which is not uncommon, lies in the deep orange colour of the columella, which contrasts with the black network of the pattern on the body whorl and the almost white aperture. Nearly all olives show a marked similarity in shape, which makes them easily recognizable. They are carnivores and live in colonies buried in sand, emerging to secure their prey, which may be living or dead. They are therefore easily captured by using bait, to the presence of which they respond very quickly, clasping the food with their foot and retreating beneath the sand to eat it. Some olives have been known to swim short distances by flapping a portion of the foot.

78 *Scientific name* Harpa major

Family Harpidae

Common name None

Size 5–9 cm.

Range Indo-Pacific and Red Sea

Harp shells, of which there are about a dozen species, are some of the loveliest of all molluscan shells. The broad, curving outline of the body whorl suggests the frame of a harp, while the numerous ribs or varices, and more especially the fine parallel lines running from shoulder to base between the ribs, emphasize the resemblance. The festoons of crescent-like markings between the glossy ribs and the rich colouring of the whole shell combine to give a wonderful effect. This is one of the common species, and was formerly often confused with *H. ventricosa*, which is restricted to the western Indian Ocean and Red Sea.

All the harps are carnivores, nocturnal and very active. The animals are so large that they cannot retreat into their shells, and will frequently amputate part of the foot to distract a predator, eventually without any difficulty growing a new portion to replace it. If the predator is a crab, the harp shell may turn the tables by instantly burying it beneath a mass of slime and sand, and then making a meal of it before it can escape.

Scientific name Harpa costata
Family Harpidae
Common name Imperial Harp
Size 6–10 cm.
Range Mauritius, Rodrigues I., and northern Madagascar

Considered a great prize by collectors of past generations, and still quite a rare and desirable shell, this species can be recognized by the large number of ribs, which are set so closely together that there is no room for any pattern between them. As in the previous species, the posterior edge of the ribs is quite sharp, and in both cases the ribs are produced into short spines at the shoulder, though in this case they are rather blunt. The coloration is rather subdued compared with other harps, consisting of greyish-brown bands which cross the cream-coloured ribs at right angles from shoulder to base. The spire, fashioned so intricately by the mollusc that it almost defies description, has a pink tip, while the glossy, creamy-white interior is tinged with gold.

80 *Scientific name* Terebra subulata

Family Terebridae

Common name Chocolate-spotted Auger

Size 5–15 cm., occasionally more

Range Indo–Pacific

The auger shells comprise one of two large families of molluscs which have these long, slender tapering shells. There are about 300 species, including many small ones, in this family alone. They are sand-dwellers and carnivorous: it is thought that their food may consist of marine worms. A poison gland is present in some species. This is a common shell, but none the less elegant in form and colour. Even better known is *T. maculata*, the Marlinspike, which is broader and much heavier with rather elongated bluish markings instead of squarish brown blotches.

The other family of long, tapering shells consists of the Turritellidae, or screw shells. With one or two exceptions, these do not have the same appeal to the average collector.

81 *Scientific name* Conus marmoreus

Family Conidae

Common name Marbled Cone

Size Up to 10 cm., exceptionally up to 15 cm.

Range Indo–West Pacific

There are believed to be over 500 species of cone shells, and the wide variety of colour patterns which they exhibit has made them firm favourites with shell-lovers the world over. This common species attracted the attention of voyagers in the tropics as early as the sixteenth century, and some Dutch paintings of the period feature this shell, which is quite unmistakable. The conical shape of the body whorl and the absence of ridges or 'teeth' in the aperture are common to all cones, but the spire in cones may be tall and tapering or completely flat, and all intermediate stages may occur in the various species or, in a few cases and to a lesser extent, within a single species. The colours of the living shell are frequently hidden beneath a periostracum (see Introduction, p. xv). There is a pure white form of the Marbled Cone.

   Some live cones, of which this is one, can inject a virulent poison, and should only be handled when wearing gloves.

82 *Scientific name* Conus imperialis

Family Conidae

Common name Imperial Cone

Size Up to 10 cm.

Range Indo–West Pacific

The term 'coronated' is applied to the spire of cones like this one, where a ring of blunt spines is present on the shoulder, and no doubt this gave rise to the name of the present species. The two broad bands of colour on the body whorl are usually present in the typical form, which is widely distributed and moderately common. The smaller shell illustrated above is the variety *fuscatus*, which is smaller, has a different pattern and is found only in Mauritius.

In many cones slight differences in pattern between individual shells are usual, yet in most cases the species or form can be identified with practice.

This species is found in sand in the vicinity of coral reefs, and feeds on polychaete worms.

83 *Scientific name*   Conus (Stephanoconus) regius

Family   Conidae

Common name   Crown Cone

Size   4–6·5 cm.

Range   Florida to Brazil and Gulf of Mexico

Quite common in the Caribbean region, there are various colour forms of this shell, three of which are illustrated above. The one on the right is the rather local form known as *citrinus*. The relationship of such widely differing forms can only be established by studying them 'in the field'. The large specimen in the centre above is still coated with its thin, brownish periostracum, which dulls the colours, though the pattern is visible through it. The small horny operculum, which is rudimentary in cones, can be seen at the top of the aperture.

  This species favours coral reefs in shallow water. The colour of the animal is said to be blood red. All cones are carnivorous, many preying on other molluscs.

84 *Scientific name* Conus (Leptoconus) ammiralis

Family Conidae

Common name Admiral Cone

Size 4–8 cm.

Range Indo–West Pacific

Few shells can boast a lovelier or more intricate colour pattern. Beside the large white tent markings which are scattered irregularly over the surface, the dark bands encircling the shell are made up of numerous fine parallel lines on which both large tents and very small white dots are superimposed, while the paler fawn-coloured portions between the dark bands are themselves made up of myriads of tiny tents. The moderately high spire, which is sometimes coronated, is covered with irregular creamy blotches. It is not a rare shell, and often occurs in fairly deep water.

A 'papillose' form, the surface covered with little knobs, is occasionally found, and goes under the name *C. architalassus*. This also is illustrated above, but one should examine it with a lens to appreciate its hidden wonders.

(Left-hand shell from the H. C. Gay collection)

85 *Scientific name* Conus (Leptoconus) generalis

Family Conidae

Common name General Cone

Size 4·5–10 cm.

Range Indo–West Pacific

There seems to be no end to the bewildering variation in colour patterns of which this rather common shell is capable, and until one has seen a large series of them one might well be forgiven for assuming that several species were represented. There are frequently three white bands encircling the shell: at the shoulder, just over halfway down the almost straight sides and at the base, the bands being dotted with brown or crossed by irregular brown lines. The shoulder is very sharp, and the spire, though flat on the outer whorls, often rises abruptly and very steeply towards the centre to form a little pointed cone. This, taken with other features, is a great help in identification.

It is frequently found in sandy areas of coral reefs in shallow water.

86 *Scientific name*   Conus (Gastridium) geographus
Family   Conidae
Common name   Geographer or Geography Cone
Size   Up to 15 cm.
Range   Indo–West Pacific

It is most important that the collector 'in the field' should be able to recognize this shell, which has with some justification been called the 'rattle-snake' of the shell world, having been directly responsible for the deaths of at least a dozen people who have handled it. The neurotoxic poison is normally used by the mollusc to kill small fish, which are its natural food, and there is no known antidote, though much research has been devoted to finding one. A small dart-like hollow tooth, through which the poison is pumped, is thrust into the victim and left there by the end of the tubular proboscis, which can extend to the full length of the shell, and the process can be repeated again and again. Death can ensue within a few hours.

The rather barrel-shaped shell, with its typical 'smudged' pattern, is light in weight and has a very wide aperture for a cone. It is an uncommon species, and does not usually occur in shallow water.

Scientific name Conus (Regiconus) aulicus
Family Conidae
Common name Court Cone
Size Up to 16·5 cm.
Range Indo–West Pacific

With its striking pattern of large white tent-markings standing out vividly against the reddish brown or sometimes almost black background, this uncommon shell contrasts sharply with the previous species, yet it too has a virulent poison which can produce severe symptoms in human beings and could possibly be lethal. The rather wide aperture is a rich creamy yellow colour, paling towards the lip, and the outside of the shell from shoulder to base is sculptured with very fine parallel ridges or 'cords', which are not obvious until the light is reflected from them. It frequents sandy patches on reefs, often being found under coral heads or stones, but usually in water of moderate depth.

88 *Scientific name* Conus (Darioconus) bengalensis

Family Conidae

Common name Glory-of-Bengal Cone

Size Up to 12 cm.

Range Bay of Bengal and Andaman Sea, in deep water

The oceans of the world contain many treasures, some still awaiting discovery, and this lovely species has provided one of the biggest sensations of recent times. It is known that one was collected in 1963, but it was not until 1968 that it was given a name and described, although by then several specimens had come to light. In March 1971 a specimen was sold by auction in London for the record price for a shell of £1,350 ($3,240). Further specimens subsequently came on the market, and in November 1972 at the same auction rooms a slightly larger specimen fetched only £25.

An allied species, the famous Glory of the Sea Cone (*C. gloriamaris*), which was once thought to be the rarest of all shells, has also been found in considerable numbers in recent years, though the price remains fairly high because of the demand from collectors.

(Shell from the J. D. Orr collection)

89 *Scientific name* Conus (Cylinder) textile

Family Conidae

Common name Cloth-of-Gold Cone; Textile Cone

Size Up to 12·5 cm.

Range Indo–Pacific

The Textile Cone is a very common and variable shell, though most specimens conform to the same general colour pattern. It is also one of the small group of really dangerous cone shells, its poison having been responsible for the deaths of at least two people. Its natural prey consists of other molluscs, including cones and cowries, and it is frequently found on reefs in shallow water, sometimes buried in sand.

This is the best-known of the 'tent cones', which are a difficult group to sort out into the various species, because they all have a somewhat similar colour pattern, and only long familiarity with their individual characteristics will make the task easier.

90 *Scientific name* Conus (Textilia) adamsonii

Family Conidae

Common name Rhododendron Cone

Size 4·5–5·5 cm.

Range Central Pacific (Cook and Phoenix Is.)

Combining the qualities of beauty and rarity, it is not surprising that this shell is so much admired by collectors. The markings do indeed bear quite a resemblance to those on some rhododendron flowers. The specimen illustrated has an interesting history, for it was in the famous Norris collection, which was sold by auction in 1873, and was purchased by Roger Gaskell of Highgate, London for £4 15s., being Lot No. 541. It was truly described in the catalogue as 'a very beautiful shell'. Roger Gaskell's priced catalogue, with his notes of his own and other purchases, is in the author's possession. A shell of which the background is known is always particularly interesting.

Scientific name Conus (Hermes) nussatella
Family Conidae
Common name Slender Cone
Size Up to 8·5 cm.
Range Indo–West Pacific

The cones of the sub-genus Hermes have rather long cylindrical shells, tapering at both ends, the spire being quite short. This is a rather common and variable species, though it is consistent in always having a large number of close-set fine ribs on the body whorl, the ribs, which may be beaded, bearing many chocolate-coloured dots or short dashes. In addition there are very irregular orange or brown markings all over the cream-coloured surface, the spire being blotched with orange and having a row of chocolate dots at the suture.

It is a coral-reef-dweller with a wide distribution in the Indo–Pacific, often being found in quite shallow water.

92 *Scientific name*   Conus (Hermes) granulatus
Family   Conidae
Common name   Glory-of-the-Atlantic Cone
Size   2·5–5 cm.
Range   Florida and the Bahamas south to Brazil

This is a lovely shell, but decidedly rare, and quite unlike any other cone on America's Atlantic coast-line. It probably occurs at depths of 60 feet or more, but nothing appears to be known of its life-history. The name *granulatus* is slightly misleading, as, although the body whorl is covered with encircling ribs which bear interrupted brown lines, there is no trace of any bead-like sculpture which could justify that name. The colour, like that of so many shells, tends to fade on exposure to light, but can be quite a bright red, the rounded whorls of the almost white spire being prettily spotted with brown, and the whitish band around the middle of the body whorl also having large brown spots around its upper edge.

93 *Scientific name* Columbarium pagoda

Family Columbariidae

Common name Pagoda Shell

Size 5–8 cm.

Range Southern coasts of Japan and Taiwan

It is interesting to speculate whether the Japanese drew the inspiration for their pagodas from this and similar shells which are to be found in the seas around their shores, but there is no direct evidence that they did so. Fossil evidence shows that shells like these were plentiful in far-off prehistoric times, but less than twenty living species linger on. Like the Latiaxis (pp. 55–7), which they somewhat resemble, they are mostly deep-water shells with little colour, though this species favours shallower water than others in the genus. The shell is thin and fragile. All pagoda shells have the very long siphonal canal and a horny operculum.

C. spinicinctum and *C. hedleyi* are somewhat similar species from Australia.

94 *Scientific name*   *Thatcheria mirabilis*

Family   Turridae

Common name   Thatcher's Wonder Shell

Size   7–10 cm.

Range   Japan, Taiwan and Philippine Is., in deep water

The exquisite lines of this thin and rather fragile shell from the depths of the ocean are unique, and their beauty is enhanced by the delicately shaded bands of colour which follow these curves on the top of the sharply keeled shoulder and on the tapering body whorl below it. From the extreme end of the keel, which, being slightly thickened, does strengthen the shell considerably, the edge of the flattened top of the aperture sweeps back in a bold curve to join the columella some distance behind. The interior is glossy white.

    This shell is not rare, but specimens are often trawled from depths of 500 feet or more where the bottom is a mixture of sand and mud, and fishing boats are the main source of supply, which does limit the numbers available.

5 *Scientific name*   *Aplustrum amplustre*

Family   Hydatinidae

Common name   Pink-banded Bubble Shell; Ship's Flag Shell

Size   1·5–2·5 cm.

Range   Indo–Pacific

Two broad pink bands outlined with black, encircling the translucent white shell, make this quite common species easily recognizable. It is very fragile, and in life the glossy shell is covered with a thin, brownish periostracum, the pattern being visible through it (bottom row). In the bubble shells the animals are normally large and very beautiful, with frilly mantle folds which can envelop the shell, as in the cowries. They are carnivorous, feeding on other molluscs.

   In a very common and closely allied species, *Hydatina physis*, the rather larger shell is cream-coloured and the pink bands are replaced by numerous parallel blackish lines, set very closely together.

96 *Scientific name*   *Papustyla pulcherrima*

Family   Helicidae

Common name   Green Tree Snail

Size   3·5–4·5 cm.

Range   Manus Island, north of New Guinea

Brilliant colours are not confined to *sea* shells, and even some of the snails in our gardens are very colourful. Green, however, is a colour which is rarely encountered, and even then it is seldom as intense a green as in this rare tree snail from the Pacific. Presumably it affords it an effective camouflage among the leaves of the trees. The colour is entirely contained in the periostracum. When this peels away, the shell beneath is seen to be white. In 1972, some forty years after it was discovered, it was declared to be an 'endangered species' because of the large number being collected, and is now protected by law: it is one of the first molluscs to be protected in this way.

97 *Scientific name*   *Polymita picta*

Family   Helicidae

Common name   Painted Snail

Size   2·5–3 cm.

Range   Only from Oriente Province, eastern Cuba

Few land snails could compete with this aptly-named species for vivid colours and varied patterns. It is hard to believe that so many designs can all be the same species, although the same thing happens with some sea shells. Thin black lines sometimes occur crossing the shell at right angles to the suture, as in the top right-hand specimen: these denote a temporary resting phase, after which growth is resumed. Like the previous species and the following one, these snails live in trees. The animal, by contrast with the shell, is very drab, being black above and grey beneath.

98 *Scientific name*   *Liguus fasciatus*

Family   Orthalicidae

Common name   Florida Tree Snail

Size   4–5 cm.

Range   Confined to the Everglades and Keys of southern Florida

There are no fewer than fifty-two named colour forms of this species, displaying a fascinating array of different patterns, the one shown here being the form *lignumvitae*. They feed on minute lichens, algae and fungi on the bark of the trees, and if transferred to a different sort of tree they will die. Many forms are nearing extinction, as their natural habitats are wiped out by property-developers and road-builders, but great efforts to conserve them are being made in the Everglades National Park. Their length of life is about three years. The molluscs are hermaphrodite, and mate in late summer, crawling down to the ground and burying their eggs in a 'nest', then ascending the trunk again and spending the ensuing dry period until the spring in a dormant state, attached to a branch.

Scientific name   Neotrigonia margaritacea
Family   Trigoniidae
Common name   Southern Brooch Shell
Size   2–4·5 cm.
Range   Tasmania, Victoria and New South Wales

The beauty of these shells lies in the delicate opalescent hues of the pearly interior, which may be silvery, tinted with pinks and greens, or sometimes a lovely rosy purple. Souvenirs such as brooches are often made from them. They are the survivors of a group of shells which abounded in early geological times, being known as fossils the world over, though now only found as living shells in Australian waters. Like the cockles, which they somewhat resemble externally, they are active creatures, living in a mud and sand environment, and using the foot to hop along on the sea-bed. The hinge has strong teeth which dovetail in a remarkable fashion and with great precision, making it difficult both to separate and to reunite the two valves. There are several other species.

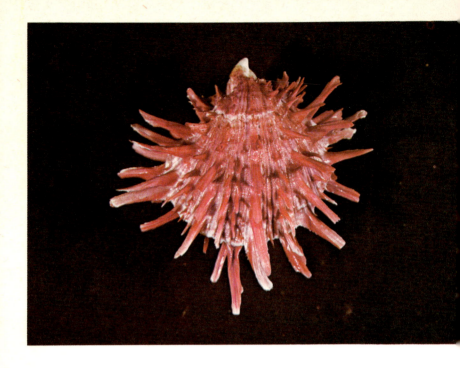

100 *Scientific name*   *Spondylus americanus*

Family   Spondylidae

Common name   Atlantic Thorny Oyster

Size   7–15 cm.

Range   Southern Florida and West Indies

'Thorny oysters' are among the most beautiful of the bivalves, many being adorned with long spines and the shells being very colourful. The common name is rather misleading, however, for they are related to the scallops and are far removed from oysters. They are sometimes known as 'Chrysanthemum Shells'. Where there are spines, these are frequently covered with marine growths, which camouflage the shell. The right valve of the shell is normally cemented to a rock, while the other is free to move: the hinge works on the ball-and-socket principle. Some seventy species have been described, but the true number is probably far less. Some lack the spines and some are very heavy, weighing as much as 9 kg., or 20 lb.

    This species is very variable in colour, and is from fairly deep water. A very similar shell from the *west* coast of America is *S. princeps*, which has rather broader, more flattened spines, not standing out at quite such an angle, but tending to follow the contour of the shell.

(Shell from the W. Karo collection)

101 *Scientific name* Gloripallium pallium

Family Pectinidae

Common name Painted Scallop

Size Up to 8·5 cm.

Range Indo–Pacific, excluding Hawaii

Scallops are some of the most familiar of all shells, and many of them are very lovely, this species being particularly admired for its beautifully sculptured ribs. These are covered along their whole length with tiny projecting scales, three abreast on the larger ribs, while very fine ridges between the ribs bear similar scales. The striking colour pattern consists of a mottling of maroon, pink or brownish shades on a cream background. The beak (see p. xviii) and the inside of the 'ears' on either side of it are frequently touched with bright orange.

This species lives below coral heads or branches, attached by a *byssus* or strand of fine threads to the corals, being found from shallow water down to about 65 feet.

102 *Scientific name* Brechites (Penicillus) pulcher

Family Clavagellidae

Common name Beautiful Watering-pot Shell

Size 7–11 cm. (disc + frill 1·5–3 cm.)

Range Indian Ocean from Mozambique to Singapore

The 'watering-pot shells' are so called because the tube with the perforated disc at the end bears a strange resemblance to the spout and rose of a watering-can. In this species the disc is surrounded by a wide 'frill', so that it looks like some strange flower. Under a lens the frill is seen to consist of a single layer of fine, hollow tubules radiating out from the centre, while the holes in the central disc are also short tubes. It is possible that water is forced out of them to enable the animal to bury itself in the mud or sand, where it lives disc downwards, the tube open at the top protecting the two siphons.

Starting life as a typical bivalve shell, this extraordinary mollusc proceeds to build this elaborate home, leaving its embryonic shell with the two valves embedded in the wall of the tube, where they are clearly visible, proving it is a bivalve. The illustration highlights the disc. The tube, which is also white, is foreshortened and in the shadow.

3 *Scientific name* Chama lazarus
Family Chamidae
Common name Lazarus Jewel Box
Size 4–12 cm.
Range Indo–West Pacific

Bearing a superficial resemblance to the 'thorny oysters', the 'jewel boxes' are nevertheless fundamentally different. They tend to have stumpy spines or flattened, leafy outgrowths rather than the delicate spines of some Spondylus, and it is usually the left valve and not the right one which is cemented to the coral or rock. The most beautiful specimens, with elaborate branching fronds, come from still water. The shells tend to become encrusted with marine organisms and to lose their beauty as they get older. This species is normally white or cream, sometimes tinged with yellow or pink, with a few reddish-brown bands spiralling outwards from the umbo. It is found on coral reefs in the tropics.

Other species, some in a wide selection of colour forms, occur in the Caribbean and elsewhere.

104 *Scientific name* Corculum cardissa
Family Cardiidae
Common name True or Broken Heart Cockle
Size Up to 7·5 cm.
Range Indo–Pacific

So perfectly does this common shell conform to the conventional heart shape that one could almost believe it was fashioned by some master craftsman of the human species. The flat, ribbed exterior of the 'heart' seems to be hollowed out on one side, except for a small raised portion below the umbos, whereas on the other side it bulges towards the centre, where the two valves meet. The shell is very thin and somewhat fragile, although the keel-like 'periphery' of the heart, which is formed by the compressed median portions of the two valves, is slightly thickened and adds considerably to the strength of the whole. This 'keel' may be smooth or edged with little spines.

The translucent shell is usually creamy-white in colour, but there are yellow and deep pink forms, and occasionally spotted ones as well. The species lives in coral-sand, in shallow water.

Scientific name Amiantis (Macrocallista) erycina

Family Veneridae

Common name None

Size 7–9 cm.

Range Aden to Indonesia and the Philippines

In the early days of shell-collecting this handsome, solid shell was considered to be one of the rarest and most desirable of all the bivalves, and it is easy to see why it was so admired. The glossy, markedly convex valves, with their closely spaced concentric grooves, are cream-coloured near the umbos, but deepen to a pale orange as they grow outwards, this colour also being present around the ligament and hinge. Two broad, wedge-shaped bands of darker colour and numerous smaller ones fan out with a slight curve across the surface. When viewed from the hinge side, the perfect symmetry of line and harmonious blend of colours are particularly pleasing.

This is one of a large family of over 400 species, known collectively as Venus Clams, with a world-wide distribution.

106 *Scientific name* Tellina radiata

Family Tellinidae

Common name Sunrise or Sunset Shell

Size 5–10 cm.

Range South-east United States and the West Indies

The glistening, smooth exterior of this colourful shell is a pale creamy white, against which the purplish pink rays which give the shell its name are displayed to advantage. On the inside of the valves these rays are often a very bright pink or red, while a large portion of the inside of each valve is often suffused with yellow. There is a white form which was once called *T. unimaculata* (also shown above). The umbos in both forms are frequently tipped with red.

This lovely and abundant species lives just below the surface on sandy shores. It may be said to symbolize the unseen and unsuspected beauty which surrounds us in so many different forms, created by these little-known creatures, the molluscs, and waiting to reward all those who seek to know more about 'the world of shells'.